with
PSC Partners Seeking a Cure

A collection of writings by Sandi Pearlman (1975-2013)
Community Relations Chair, PSC Partners Seeking a Cure

Compiled and Edited by Mike Pearlman
Photographs by K Pearlman Photography

TABLE OF CONTENTS

SANDI'S JOURNEY WITH PSC PARTNERS SEEKING A CURE

This is a story about a young woman, Sandi Pearlman, who was diagnosed with primary sclerosing cholangitis (PSC), a rare liver and bile duct disease, and her involvement with PSC Partners Seeking a Cure (PSC Partners), a 501(c)3 non-profit foundation dedicated to helping those with this disease. Through Sandi's writings, we hope to share her journey, a journey of support, education, friendship, inspiration and love.

The Disease – the National Institutes of Health (NIH) describes PSC as "a disease that damages and blocks bile ducts inside and outside the liver. Bile is a liquid made in the liver. Bile ducts are tubes that carry bile out of the liver to the gallbladder and small intestine. In the intestine, bile helps break down fat in food. . . . In PSC, inflammation of the bile ducts leads to scar formation and narrowing of the ducts over time. As scarring increases, the ducts become blocked. As a result, bile builds up in the liver and damages liver cells. Eventually, scar tissue can spread throughout the liver, causing cirrhosis and liver failure." (http://www.niddk.nih.gov/health-information/health-topics/liver-disease/primary-sclerosing-cholangitis/Pages/facts.aspx, accessed November 8, 2014.)

Most people, including many medical practitioners, have not heard of, or have little familiarity with PSC. In the United States, it is estimated that there are 29,000 people who have this disease.

PSC is a scary diagnosis. While the causes of PSC are not known, it is thought that genes, immune system problems, bacteria and viruses may be involved. Among the PSC symptoms are an intense, unitchable itching (described by some as having fireants under your skin), extreme fatigue that rest will not fix, pain in the upper right part of the abdomen, chills and fever, and a yellowing of the skin and eyes (jaundice). At the current time, the disease is incurable and there is no effective treatment, other than a liver transplant, and even then PSC can re-appear.

The Organization – PSC Partners Seeking a Cure (www.pscpartners.org) was started in 2005 by Ricky Safer (a person with PSC, a "PSCer") and her husband Don. PSC Partners mission is to provide education and support to persons with PSC, to their families and caregivers; and to raise funds to research causes, treatments and cures for PSC. PSC Partners also supports organ donation awareness. In support of its research mission, PSC Partners has awarded over $1.5 million dollars. The research funds are allocated by PSC Partners Scientific/Medical Advisory Committee (SMAC), which includes world-renowned PSC physicians and researchers. PSC Partners also holds an annual conference for education and support, and has become the largest gathering of PSC patients and caregivers in the world. These conferences are affiliated with PSC academic, medical and research centers, including the University of Pittsburgh Medical Center, Northwestern University School of Medicine, the University of Colorado Hospital, the Liver Center of Yale University, the UC Davis School of Medicine, and the Mayo Clinic.

--

Growing up, Sandi frequently experienced nausea, vomiting and fatigue, which were "treated" with various medications. At the age of 31 (in 2007) she was diagnosed with primary sclerosing cholangitis. In early 2007, Sandi was working her evening shift at the Central Rappahannock Regional Library, having driven herself to work earlier that day. At the end of her shift, she called us (her parents) in Chantilly, Virginia, asking if we would drive the 40 miles to the library and take her home. Sandi said she felt unable to drive. Looking back, I wish we had agreed, but we did not. Instead we encouraged her to drive herself the 15-20 miles to her home in Fredericksburg, Virginia. Getting off the phone, Sandi called her sister Karen who drove to the library and took Sandi home.

For all practical purposes, Sandi never drove again. She went to see a new doctor who had been recommended to her by friends. The doctor, whose focus is internal medicine, ran some tests and made medical referrals. Over the next few months, Sandi's conditioned worsened and she was admitted into Georgetown University Hospital. It was at Georgetown that her diagnosis of primary sclerosing cholangitis was confirmed.

The above events took place around the time of the PSC Partners Seeking a Cure 2007 conference. We momentarily thought about trying to attend, but Sandi was not interested, and we were uncertain. Our journey with PSC Partners thus began in earnest in 2008. Over the next six years, Sandi went from a person who had to be "dragged" to her first conference in Jacksonville, Florida (2008), to a person who would <u>insist</u> on attending what turned out to be her last conference in Pittsburgh, Pennsylvania (2013). Sandi passed away in November 2013.

What follows is a snapshot of Sandi's involvement with PSC Partners from initial reluctance to passion and commitment, and of an organization that gave her the freedom to do this. This book is divided into seven parts, largely consisting of excerpts from Sandi's writings. The complete writings are provided at the end of the book, under "Reference Cites."

Part 1 contains Sandi's descriptive articles, with titles like "Sanity Street" and "There's a Song in my Heart," for each of the PSC Partners Conferences she attended. The articles focus primarily on the emotional support provided, as she writes about "the warmth of the attendees," "the feeling that you're no longer alone," and how "PSC Partners conferences are a love letter of sorts." Part 2 continues this theme, with her writings (for example, "It's All About the Nap" and "The Glass Half Full") focusing on areas of interest to PSCers who are in their 20s and 30s, e.g., going to parties, dating, romance and work. As Sandi wrote, "Just at a time when we're supposed to be exploring ourselves, going out, meeting people, we PSCers face an energy crisis."

Part 3 covers programs in which Sandi was actively involved, programs like Save the Day (annual fundraiser), Mentor-Mentee, Newcomer Orientation, and Facebook, each one directed to how we help one another, how we are "together in the fight." Part 4 reflects our desire to make lists, with Sandi writing about "The Happiness Plan" (for example, "Every once in a bit, let the fatigue monster win, but on your terms") and the "Top Ten Reasons to Attend . . . [a] PSC Partners Conference" (reason number 5, "Scratch, itch, nap in peace").

Part 5 has entries on several topics, such as spirituality, describing this as "anything and everything that makes you feel connected and a bit freer from the everyday stressors of your world." There also are segments on "Family and Laughter," highlighting the importance of each, and on various Facebook threads covering topics of interest to those with PSC and their caregivers. These threads run the gamut from the more serious topics, such as "Quality of Life" and "Asking for Help" to the more humorous, but still very important topics, such as "I so hate it when… (because we all need a place to laugh and vent! :)." This part also has a section titled,

"PSC Stands For. . . ." We all know that PSC is a serious disease, but through humor, Sandi and others have offered alternative connotations for those letters, such as "Pretty Sexy Chicks," "Please Send Chocolate," and "Patient Spending Club." Part 5 closes with "A Few of My PSC Things," a song written by Sandi to describe her PSC and the benefits of PSC Partners Seeking a Cure.

Part 6 gives a snapshot of how Sandi was seen "Through the Eyes of Others." In describing Sandi, it was written, "Help others, that was key to her being. Help others lovingly....She changed the world one day at a time and had the ability to transfer all her joy to each one of us."[1] Part 7, "Closing Comments," uses Sandi's own words to describe who she was, "I'm no longer who I used to be. . . . But I'm a warrior. I'm a fighter and an educator. . . . I'm a survivor. And if my disease takes me tomorrow, it will be on my terms. . . . I won't cease to exist. Who I was, what I did, those questions may still be asked. The answers? My answers? More researchers and doctors and civilians will know the name PSC and will realize there is a war to win than before I came. . . ."

I have asked myself why I wanted to compile her writings, and believe there are two reasons. The first is that Sandi was a wonderful writer, with the ability to colorfully describe her topic, whether reasons for attending a PSC Partners Conference, or issues impacting those in their 20s and 30s, or new endeavors such as starting a Facebook support group and an annual Save the Day fundraiser. My second reason is from once asking Sandi, a person very content with staying home, reading a good book, and watching television, why she was so open to sharing within the world of PSC Partners. Her response was simple - those with PSC and their caregivers (including herself and her family) needed to share with, and to gain support from, one another. By being so open herself, she hoped this would encourage others to do the same. With that in mind, may this collection of Sandi's writings help others in their fight against this insidious disease.

PART 1 – PSC PARTNERS CONFERENCES
(From "I didn't want to go" to "Thank you")

2008 – Sandi's First Conference

Our first impression of Sandi at the 2008 annual PSC Partners conference in Jacksonville was that of a quiet young woman who appeared reluctant to step into an environment that was defined by disease. At the end of the three days, little did we know that, within a year, she would become a shining star of PSC Partners and the voice of PSCers.[1]

Sandi did not want to go to her first Conference. She and I (her father) drove from Virginia to the conference in Jacksonville, Fla. During the ride, Sandi laid in the back seat of the car, occasionally "sharing" her view on how she was not happy about what was taking place. As she later described it, "I'll tell you the truth, I didn't want to go. I couldn't stand the thought of being stuck in a room with a bunch of sick people and talking nonstop about feeling terrible and all the rest. I wanted to hide under the covers and cry."[2]

Sandi expanded on these feelings in 2011, ". . . before my first conference I'd never met another PSCer. Honestly, I didn't even particularly want to meet another PSCer. I was symptomatic, a bit angry and unwilling to take a leap into *a whole new world*. I was pretty darn certain that if the sun was going to come up tomorrow, I'd probably be burned to a crisp instead of basking in its warm vitamin D bestowing glow. I'd never been a pessimist before, but I was well on my way."[3]

As it turned out, Sandi's first contact with a "PSCer" was in the parking lot as we arrived at the Jacksonville Conference. As she was getting out of the car, she met Ricky and Don Safer, who also were getting out of their car. As Sandi described it, ". . . I got out of the car and ran into Ricky and Don Safer about one minute after I arrived. Ricky's the PSCer, but there she was practically sparkling with warmth and radiation and buzzing with energy. Don had a mischievous twinkle in his eye and a hug and a grin that made me feel instantly safe and part of a family. I was still wary but less so."[2]

At the start of her first Conference, Sandi was asked to help out with the registration process. This gave her the opportunity to interact with others. As Sandi later wrote, "As the weekend wore on, I realized that warmth and sharing and frivolity made the hard stuff easier to bear and by the end of my time there [at the Conference], I truly had made lifelong friends and found a new purpose to my heretofore meaningless days."[2]

2009

In 2009, Sandi attended her second PSC Partners Conference, this time in Chicago, Illinois. She wrote the following about her experience:

Once More With Feeling: My Return Trip to the PSC Partners Seeking a Cure Conference[4]

The thing I love most about life-altering experiences is that even when you expect them, they can still turn out to surprise you with the myriad of ways they can touch your heart.

I mean, I knew my first PSC Partners Conference had made me into a much-improved person from the shell-shocked PSCer who walked through the doors that first Friday afternoon. I'd been given confidence, a purpose, friendships that have stood the tests of time and frequent hospitalizations.

So, when Chicago rolled around, for months on end I proudly stepped forward and touted the glories of the conference to every prospective attendee for so long and as loud as I could. I figured I knew, so to speak, what I was getting into, what would await others. I mean, I was no longer a first timer.

I already knew about the warmth of the attendees, the staggering intellect of the speakers and PSCers combined, the sheer breadth of topics covered and even a good number of the people I would see. My goal for this year's Chicago conference was to help make sure others got that life-changing experience and to sort of live it vicariously through them.

And then I arrived and realized that life changing isn't just once in a lifetime and it's not just for those who have never been part of a PSC Partners Conference before.

To be honest, I'm not sure when it hit me. It may have been when the first attendees started wandering the halls. It may have been as we were packing up and preparing goody bags to hand out. It doesn't really matter. All that matters is that suddenly, I was at ease.

I felt relaxed and happy and whole. I wasn't the sick girl in the room. I wasn't the one people were whispering about with the rare incurable disease. I wasn't even the only one exhausted and scratching and itching and forgetting my words before they could come out of my mouth.

I was just in a room with a bunch of people like me who were proudly wearing their blue dots (PSCers) and their yellow dots (caregivers) and their red dots (first-timers) and green ones (transplant) all declaring that we were members of the same group, of the same family – that we were the ones who belonged. . . .

2010

In 2010, the PSC Partners Conference was held in Hartford, Connecticut. In early summer 2010, Sandi wrote the following:

The Conference: Magic, Family and Love[5]

There's a song by The Lovin' Spoonful that starts, "Do you believe in Magic [....] How the music can free her, wherever it starts . . ." And regardless of your mood, you sort of find yourself humming along and a bit peppier when those opening chords strike no matter your age or disposition or even musical leanings. I mean, true, when it's stuck in your head and won't leave it's not quite so magical, but I digress.

In any case, I dare to say that The Lovin' Spoonful had never heard of PSC and I'm utterly positive that they've never attended a PSC Partners Conference, and, yet, their upbeat, infectious, grin-inducing song perfectly encapsulates the magnetic kind of magic that emerges as soon as you cross the threshold into conference territory and take in your very first PSCer. . . .

. . . . It's that feeling that you're no longer alone.

You're not an outsider. For a few sweet, all-too-short days, you're—we're—not the other. We don't have to explain anything because to be too tired to carry on a conversation or so itchy that you can't stop scratching is the status quo. There's no explanation that you're fatigued and what that means. We know. We get it. . . .

Here's what is: Suddenly, we're not PSCers with whispered tones. We're PSCers loud and proud and, quite frankly, the envy of many of the others in the room. We're the cool kids. We're the trendsetters and we're the norm. We relish our time together. We don't need words or labels or descriptions to understand. We just know.

Having PSC gives us a shorthand that defies the need for vocabulary. We're greedy for our time together. When the days' events end, we're still just beginning. It's when we're most free to put on our baggiest sweats and pull on our baseball caps and break out the ponytail holders and slippers. It's when we share the stories of our lives, the real details: we talk husbands, wives, lovers, friends, kiddos, pets, movies and all the rest; but we also talk pain, emotional and physical, and tell our medical stories, what led to diagnosis or a new medicine we've tried that works so well we actually get why we take it. Sometimes we cry, heaving sobs that require arms around the shoulders and a group hug.

Mostly though, we laugh. We talk and we listen. We gather in groups big and small and float in and out of conversations. . . .

We're stronger physically and emotionally. Our bonds are renewed and our faith in ourselves restored.

Some of us talk. We get it all out where we know we're safe and loved and our words are strong and taken in and kept close to everyone's hearts and confidences. But it's not even about being able to say the words yourself.

There are those of us who are still afraid to speak, too newly diagnosed to voice our deepest fears and, yet, when somebody else does it's the most heartbreaking, beautiful, freeing kind of pain you can imagine. Suddenly, something that preys on you, makes monsters out of the shadows in your mind is vanquished. No matter the fear, chances are another PSCer has it, has had it, or understands it.

Here, in the confines of the conference, of our newfound family, secrets are safe and fears hold no power. Alone, we're afraid, but together we're strong. . . .

2011

In 2011, the Conference was held in Sacramento, California. As might be clear by now, Sandi enjoyed using musical references in her writings, and this is clearly shown from these excerpts:

Sanity Street[6]

Do you remember the opening song to Sesame Street? It goes something like this: "Sunny day, sweepin' the clouds away. On my way to where the air is sweet."

I mean, sure, in the case of the song it's all about how to get to Sesame Street. But I think we can co-opt it a bit and substitute "Sanity Street" instead.

Because the lyrics to the song are so fitting it's almost like they were written for a PSC Partners conference. The air is sweet and everything is always A-Okay when we're together. . . .

Too often PSC can make us feel like we're in the shadows, like we have to search for sunlight and happiness. We're others. We're alone and we're trying to navigate a world in which we're the Oscar the Grouches of Sesame Street, the ones who are always left out of the fun and freedom the rest of the world so easily enjoys. . . .

At a PSC Partners conference, there's just no chance to feel like an outsider. We come from all over the world and speak many different languages. We're in all stages and all have different levels of knowledge about PSC and what it means. Some of us are well-informed, some of us just beginning our PSCer journeys. It doesn't make a difference.

Upon walking in, the love is so overwhelming that there's no chance to feel estranged or removed and the warmth is so empowering that we simply can't shut our lids tight and not experience it all.

Whether we itch or can't get through the day without a nap or a caregiver, there's somebody else who not only gets it but who lives it. There are real-life experiences, answers, empathy and compassion and it's all there just for all of us. . . .

Every conference includes experts in the field and this one is no different. We've got doctors from a renowned PSC clinic attending, researchers who are dedicated to helping us unravel the mysteries of PSC, experts in hepatology. We have psychologists who know the best ways in which we can help ourselves understand the enigma of our illness and what PSC is doing to our bodies and minds.

We have physicians and PSCers alike who are all too ready and willing to share the ways in which we can be proactive and ask all the right questions of our medical facilities back home.

We have question and answer panels and a chance to make our voices heard. We discuss the ups and downs of searching for a cure and all the aspects that worry us and bring us cheer when it comes to discoveries that are being made every single day. All of this is vitally important.

But perhaps even more so, we're together, PSCers and caregivers. We laugh and we cry. There may occasionally be tears streaming down our faces but also laughter so loud that it's hard to believe that we're an alcohol free group dealing with the realities of a disease for which there is really no known treatment or a cure as of yet.

We're free to be ourselves in a way that is judgment free and unavailable anywhere else on the planet. Every cell, every breath, every thought is lit up with love and understanding and when there's fear or doubt or worry, there are hundreds of willing shoulders to lean on and arms to wrap around you.

It's okay to be a PSCer. It's okay to be scared. It's okay to be you, no matter what that means. . . .

Oh, and the best part: our version of Sesame Street, is without end. It stretches from Israel to Australia, Louisiana to Victoria, Stockholm to South Dakota and Florida to Fiji. It's without end and we've definitely got room for you on our street and in our lives.

Sandi's song references went full tilt in early summer 2011:

There's a Song in my Heart[3]

Okay. I admit it. I'm a musical junkie. *Singing in the Rain, Thoroughly Modern Millie, Mama Mia, Rent*, I could go on and on and...well, okay, on. But before you write me off as some musical loving goonie, bear with me a bit because here's the thing: in a musical, there's escape from the world in a way that just isn't generally offered in real life. In musicals, when something terrible happens, as it often does, there are still songs to sing, hugs to share or catchy anthems to occupy us as the tears roll down our collective cheeks. Musicals aren't just movie experiences, they're visceral ones. Even decades after watching a film, hearing the first few bars of the score transports us back. It's kind of like our very own time machines traveling *across the universe* granting instant access to memories, emotions and experiences. Honestly, even you nonmusical enthusiasts must admit to occasionally finding yourself humming along to a theme song or two--right? I mean, who among us hasn't been whisked away to *Bali Hai* or wondered exactly how to spell *Supercalifragilisticexpialidocious* at least once or twice a year? And although the conferences you see in movies (Rosie's sexy dance in *Bye, Bye, Birdie* anyone?) vary quite a bit from anything you'll find at a PSC Partners' conference--although this year we did include bull riding, so never say never-- still, they put a song in my heart like I'm *singing in the rain*. So, going with that, ahem, theme, here are a few of *my favorite things* about PSC Partners conferences and the memories and realities they make:

You'll Never Walk Alone.

Diagnosis of a rare disease which most people--heck, most doctors--have never heard of is downright terrifying. Like *Thoroughly Modern Millie's* Mrs. Meers is forever saying, "Sad to be all alone in the world." And it is...only, we're not. Let me emphasize that. We are NOT all alone in the world and there's no place in the universe that is more proof positive of that than a PSC Partners conference. . . .

So many of us walking through the doors of our first conference feel as kicked about and alone as Little Orphan Annie. We've discovered we are PSCers in a non-PSC world and feel it's practically a given that it's going to be *a hard-knock life*. For many, information on their disease has been scarce or nonexistent and, for an alarming number, just downright wrong. So, if you entered your first conference feeling much more *I shall scream* than *I think I'm gonna like it here* or those feelings have kept you from attending, rest assured, you're not alone. But like any good musical, there's a silver lining to be found and attending the conference guarantees...

The Sun'll Come Up Tomorrow.

You can bet your bottom dollar on that, no wishing on a star needed. No matter what life throws at us, and we all know far too well that life can be a big, old bully at times, shining a light on each other and on ourselves really does make all the difference. We don't have to live in the shadows, vampire-like victims of a dreaded disease. PSC is hard. Conferences can be hard. This one was hard at times and the next one will likely be hard at times, too. We don't have a disease with simple answers or very many solutions. The temptation to drown in ourselves and our situations can be downright enticing and to say a conference saved me is at once true and far too pat. But I can tell you that the decision to attend, for me and for so many other PSCers I speak with, helps us *[get] out of bed on the right side*. And because of that, even when we're feeling lousy, it's still a pretty wonderful day. . . .

Somewhere Out There.

Because that's the thing, we are together no matter the distance. We don't need Doris Day singing *Que Sera Sera* or the confines of a certain city to maintain our newly formed and newly reinvigorated bonds because they're more than a fleeting fancy. They're not just yearbook promises to be BFFs 4-ever. In big things and small, fun and not so fun, we've got each other's backs, fronts, livers and lives and we're well aware of *what a beautiful morning* it is. A first-time attendee mentioned he was having his first procedure a week after the conference. You know what happened? He got cards and flowers and visits from PSCers who just two weeks beforehand he hadn't even met. There were names on some of his cards that he didn't even recognize without turning to the conference photos for some help. We're not just *people who need people*, we're PSCers who need each other and when we say *I'd do anything*, we mean it.

When I was stuck in the hospital over Thanksgiving, my favorite holiday, hundreds of my conference pals spent their time making apple turkeys and sending me pics by Facebook just to give me a smile. There are scores of stories, volumes and tomes that even *Marian the librarian* would have trouble keeping up with and cataloging. . . . We're announcing we get by...

With a Little Help From [our] Friends.

. . . . Whether connecting on Facebook or phone, in person or at a hospital, we refuse to simply say *Goodnight, Sweetheart* when a conference must finally come to an all-too-soon end. . . . I don't have a day go by that I don't hear from a member of my PSC family. And that makes me an incredibly blessed girl. And it's not just me that's staying connected. So, I'm asking...

Take a Chance on Me.

I beg you. Not just me, but on you as well. *We are family.* So, *let's get together*, yeah? I know I'm asking a lot of some of you to put your faith in me and in PSC Partners. I'm asking you to *follow the yellow brick road*--and no, that's not a jaundice joke--because at the end is something even better than Oz; it's a place where you not only find that you possess a heart, a brain and more courage than a den full of lions. It's a place where in one weekend, a few short hours, you can change your life. It's so much more than *a spoonful of sugar* designed to mask the bitter and the tough. It's a place where you know you *must've done something good.* So whether you can get behind pulling down curtains to somehow garner enough fabric for 7 children's playclothes or simply can't fathom the thought that anybody would name their child *Truly Scrumptious*, just remember that for so many, for me, when our annual PSC Partners conference ends each year, it says so much more than *so long, farewell*. We might have tears in our eyes. We might have lumps in our throats. We might be more than a bit weepy about the thought of waking up tomorrow and not seeing the faces of those who love us, understand us and have become as much a part of our systems as our own breath over the course of the weekend. But we also are saying *Good Morning* to a whole new life, one in which there's definitely something to sing about.

So from me to you, thank you for being *the wind beneath my wings* and for teaching me and helping me to teach others that *[we] can fly*. Until next conference, there's a song in my heart and a bluebird on my shoulder...and if you don't know what that means, well, you've clearly got some musicals to watch. . . .

2012

In 2012, the PSC Partners Conference was held in Rochester, Minnesota, and Sandi felt fortunate to have been asked to serve as the Conference co-chair. Prior to the conference, Sandi, continuing her theme of music, television shows or the like, wrote the following:

Three Cheers for PSC Partners Conferences![7]

Did you ever watch that old TV show, "Cheers," the one with Sam and Diane, Carla, Cliff and Norm? It's about a bunch of people whose lives revolve around a bar...at least on the surface. Okay. I know, I know, you're already thinking I've flipped my lid writing about a TV show based on a bar in a PSC newsletter of all places, but bear with me for a second.

Because, you see, while Cheers was, in fact, about a group of (perhaps) high-functioning alcoholics and those who waited on them, it was also about a family, people who loved each other and really got each other even when the outside world didn't play fair. . . .

You see, in the real world, I'm the other. I need a transplant. I have a rare disease. I itch. I'm swollen. I can't sleep and my brain occasionally forgets helpful things like where I am or what I've been doing or the word for "cat." But at the conference, none of that matters. I'm not the other. I'm one and the same in the best of all possible ways. And you know what, you will be, too.

In a world where everyone is constantly judging everyone else, the conference is this lovely oasis in the storm. . . . You can scratch, need daytime naps, forget your words and even pass out (although we'd much prefer you conscious) and nobody will judge you. If you happen to be having one of those days where you scratch until you bleed, you won't find judgment or even pity at a [PSC Partners] conference. Instead, you're much more likely to find the person next to you offering up a tissue and commiserating about how awful it is to feel like fireants have taken up residence just under your skin. One look at a conference agenda will tell you that PSC is no laughing matter. Our topics range the scope from genetics to MELD, CCA to Urso, Transplant and Depression and back and forth and everywhere in between. But lest you feel as though the conference is just about the tough and cold, hard facts of having an incurable illness, let me let you in on another little secret. PSC Partners conferences are also notorious for their laughter and fun. . . .

Following the Conference, Sandi again spoke of the strength that one can get from attending a conference:

The Love Letter[8]

. . . . And for me, for many, PSC Partners conferences are a love letter of sorts. It's all of us, taking time from our overly busy and hectic lives and putting down obstacles and illnesses and demands to be with each other come what may. For we know, this all-too-short weekend is our chance to profess our love and dedication to one another and our commitment to curing not just ourselves, but all of us. We're together in the fight, whatever it takes, not because it's the PSC Partners slogan; but because it describes what's written in our hearts and souls, in our very cells. It is the essence of a love letter, eternal, beautiful, powerful. . . .

. . . .There's simply no such thing as isolation at the conference. From the hugs and greetings as one enters the door to the handholding and tissue sharing in breakout groups or as we listen to sometimes dire statistics, the love is there. It bubbles out in song--lots of songs this year--and in stories and in shared moments. It's there in the knowledge that our loads are much lighter because we have everyone's shoulders to share the weight and it's no longer our battle alone. . . .

2013

In 2013, Sandi attended what turned out to be her final PSC Partners Conference, in Pittsburgh, Pennsylvania. At first, she wasn't sure she was going to go, writing:

To Conference or Not to Conference[9]

I wasn't going to go. If you know me, you know that's no small thing. I half expect when the vampires take my blood one of these days that I'll get a call saying, "Um, you know, we're wondering something. You see, our techs are finding all these little *PSC Partners* floating in your bloodstream like some kind of madcap chicken soup...."

Why? Well, I wasn't sure I had it in me, physically, emotionally or otherwise. I was just plain, old spent. . . . Plus, how was I going to enjoy myself, run my sessions, do all I needed to do when I'm so far past empty that the red line gave up on the gauge and called out for pizza instead? But, pal, boy am I glad I went and here's why: You all rock. We rock. PSCers are amazingly extraordinary people and stunningly wonderful in so many ways. . . .

At the conference, it doesn't matter if you're 13 or 33, 40 or 75, we're all the same, even in our differences because we choose, on a level not even our subconscious recognizes as decision making, to recognize each other. During sessions, we devour information and look to the experts to fill gaps in our knowledge or teach us something new. Out of the sessions, we sing (boy, do we ever) and we shop and we savor each moment because we know how fleeting they are. Those of us who normally sleep 18 hours a day or can't get up off the couch are suddenly going out to get sandwiches at 2:00 a.m. because we can't bear the thought of missing a moment. We literally exhaust ourselves for that one more second to spend together. . . .

So, I thank you. Thank all of you. Because, you see, you've restored me. You've given me strength to take with me and memories to keep me laughing (anyone who missed Karaoke, please, don't make that mistake again!). When I go into my next appointment, I'm not walking in alone. You're there with me, holding my hand and whispering words of encouragement. And when the news isn't good and I want to cry, your shoulders are ready for me to lean on. We're never in this thing all alone because we have each other. . . .

PART 2 – THE 20-30-SOMETHINGS

Sandi attended her first PSC Partners Conference in the spring of 2008. That fall, she began writing articles for the PSC Partners newsletter, The Duct. Over the next few years, Sandi wrote many articles, on a wide variety of topics.

One of her first columns dealt with "The 20–30-Somethings." Being young herself, Sandi saw this area as having special concerns, for example, leaving home for the first time, and going to parties and bars, as well as dating, romance and work. Her columns and the PSCers 20s-30s conference support groups provided for an open discussion of concerns. Below are several columns specifically relating to this group.

In her first The 20-30-Somethings column ("It's All About the Nap"), Sandi wrote about some of the "hot topics" facing this age group but, not surprisingly, she offered no solutions. Sandi's strength and desire in much of her writing was less on problem-solving and more about helping others by sharing, educating, keeping an honest but positive attitude and, above all else, about loving.

It's All About the Nap[10]

It's hard enough to be in your 20s and 30s. Everyone tells you that they're the greatest times of your life: you leave home for the first time, you find a job, contemplate starting a family with that special someone, etc. It's a lot for anyone to deal with. And then you add PSC. Wet blanket, anyone?

Just at a time where we're supposed to be exploring ourselves, going out, meeting people, we PSCers face an energy crisis.

In our 20s, we're experiencing college, leaving home and living on our own for the first time. It's a time to go wild, to be free to try a million different things on the path to finding out who we are. You're supposed to fall in love with all the wrong people, shut down bars and parties, hang out at diners until the wee hours of the morning.

Only problem is, you can't seem to stay up past 8:00, you're so tired that holding a conversation is tantamount to climbing Mt. Everest and the only bedroom activity you're interested in involves you, your comforter, and some nice long Zzzzs.

As to those trips to the local bar, well, you're pretty sure eventually somebody's going to notice that the only drink that ever touches your hand is an orange soda or a rum and coke minus the rum. And pick-up lines: "Hi, I'm Jack, I can't drink, I feel the need to sleep for hours on end, I itch in the oddest places and, oh, yeah, I have an incurable disease that will most likely lead to transplant. How about I buy you a coke?"

In our 30s, we're supposed to be settling down, solidifying our careers, making lifelong commitments and starting families. Our peers are happy to trot along to the local bar for a quick pint and not make it home 'til five past midnight while we're struggling to stay awake for the 7:00 news or fighting our urge to just let the kids forage in the pantry for whatever they may find and call it dinner surprise. And that's just for those of us who even have the energy to work, leave the house or have kids.

A quick drink with the boss seems like the road to promotion, but how to explain why that's just not quite possible without giving your boss details best left private or being labeled a recovering alcoholic or prude.

And let us not forget the romantic side of things. First, we have to have the energy to go out and meet someone, not to mention hold a sparkling conversation if and when we do.

Then, that partner has to remain unfazed by the whole transplant thing and, on top of that, be more than a little understanding when we're just too tired to be in the mood. If you know someone who fits this description and has decent health insurance, by all means, send him my way and check to see how many siblings he has for the rest of us out there.

Here's the thing, it's cute to have nap time when you're in kindergarten. It's fine for execs to power nap in the afternoon. It's not so fine when you're so exhausted all the time that your version of a nap lasts three or four hours and you're still exhausted upon waking.

So, what's a PSCer to do? Do we proudly wear Ts that shout slogans like "I [heart] Naps" or warn our dates, spouses, and friends that if we fall asleep on them it really isn't the company? Should we all hang out with narcoleptics so they just won't notice?

I guess there are no easy answers, at least none that I can come up with at the moment and it is getting close to nap time . . .

In the Spring of 2009, Sandi spoke directly to her situation in "The Glass Half Full." In her writing (and in her life), Sandi showed not only an awareness of the reality that she was facing, but also of her spirit and positive outlook. The sadness that most clearly came through in her column was not her medical health, but rather the "jaundiced" view of the health care professional, those who appear to believe the absence of <u>complete</u> sadness on the part of a PSCer means you are not facing up to your situation. [I recall attending one conference where a mental health professional told the attendees that a person with PSC was depressed, and needed therapy. There was a complete absence of recognizing the individuality of the person.]

The Glass Half Full[11]

As I'm sitting here writing this, I am mere hours away from my 33rd birthday. I suppose I could be out whooping it up, drowning the last of 32 in glasses of wine and beer held aloft by well-wishing friends and family.

. . . . To look at me, I look like an average girl, perhaps a little too thin, maybe in need of a haircut, but rather unremarkable all the same. No one would ever look at me and think, well, that girl there is fighting an incurable disease.

And yet, that's exactly what I am doing, what we are really doing (minus the girl for some of us!). We're fighters. We're given an impossible task: beat an incurable disease and live life without letting it destroy us, and, still, we march on.

I had a pre-interview with one of the counselors on my transplant team. For those of you who haven't yet had the pleasure, they ask you a lot of questions, try to gauge how emotionally ready you'll be when and if the big day comes, freak you out about finances and planning and that kind of a thing.

In any case, my counselor (who would have a conniption if she read this and found I called her "counselor" rather than case worker or social worker) asked me what was the best thing that ever happened to me.

I responded that it probably hadn't happened yet. She frowned and asked me, well, what's the worst thing that ever happened to you. I said, well, it probably hasn't happened yet. Her response, I swear, was that she thinks I need therapy.

See, she couldn't understand why I wouldn't say PSC was the worst thing that ever happened to me. She couldn't grasp why it wasn't waiting there on the tip of my tongue like a cat after cheese and eager to drop from my lips. But the truth is, I find my answer hopeful that there's more to come, that PSC isn't the defining characteristic of my life.

Don't get me wrong, PSC sucks. . . . But the fact is, in some ways PSC is both one of the best and one of the worst things in my life.

Before you all scream that the therapy idea was right, let me explain. The itching, nausea, RUQ pain, shortened life expectancy, etc., is more than a drag. It absolutely has to be worse than Chinese water torture.

But PSC also gives us an edge. We're not like the dude on the couch in the lounge somewhere thinking he has an unlimited lifetime to make choices and say sorry and make love and dream dreams. We know life is precious. It's ours for this day and hopefully for the next and, damn, if we're going to waste it. . . .

Well, the truth is, there are days when I want to curl up in a corner and whine why me and bawl my eyes out until I've lost at least four pounds of water weight. But what's the use?

At the end of the day, unless you've got a better connection to God than I do, you're probably not going to get an answer. So, as 33 rapidly approaches, instead of wallowing in the have-nots of being sick and lacking energy and facing what could be years of poking and prodding and ERCPs and colonoscopies and the like, I find myself smiling.

I still may need therapy, but PSC has taught me to appreciate what is good. I know who my true friends are, I feel the warmth and the love as they and my family rally around me. I laugh as they jokingly refer to PSC as Pearlman, Sandi Cure. I think, all in all, I'm a lucky girl.

I may have a disease that requires a fight every single day of my life, I may be on a first name basis with more doctors than I can shake a stick at and have my own shelf in the pharmacy, but it also allows me to see all the things worth fighting for that might otherwise have gone unnoticed. . . .

I can be me without worrying what the world will think because I know every moment is precious and there's no guarantee that tomorrow will be there...and if it is and I'm itching and exhausted, well, I know I've survived it before and I'll most likely survive it again today.

That summer, Sandi's column spoke specifically to the value of being able to interact with others of your age, facing similar concerns.

Once More with Feeling:
My Return Trip to the PSC Partners Seeking a Cure Conference[4]

. . . . It seemed no matter where in the room you looked, there was another 20/30 something. We were there. We were listening. We were in this together. . . .

One of my beautiful PSC pals said to me, you know, I feel like you're all my best friends who I can share everything and anything with, even though I only get to see you once a year or so. And she's right. . . .

There is such a safety in the room, in that group of individuals. There's no hiding of symptoms or exhaustion. There's no embarrassment or accusation. There's just overwhelming support and love and understanding. . . .

Some of what we heard at the conference was rough. Some speakers hammered us over and over again with the fact that many of us might likely die before we'd ever get a cadaveric donor. Some spoke about trials that we'd had our hearts and minds invested in as though they were somewhat laughable.

And some validated us. One speaker in particular spoke of the exhaustion that pervades so many of our lives and told us that exhaustion is real, that we're not lazy. That exhaustion is mental, physical, emotional and pervasive. I know several 20s/30s who would have stood up and applauded at this, you know, had they not been so exhausted. . . .

But for most of us, no matter how fabulous the speakers are (and they are) or how many statistics and studies are named, the true healing and education comes not in the doctors' speeches or through the painstakingly made presentations. No, those educate. Those give us food for thought. But those aren't the true reason that the conference means what it does.

Quite simply, it's the togetherness. Whether through breakout groups or just hanging out in hotel lobbies, the real miracle of the conference for all of us, at least in the 20s/30s group, is each other.

For those of you who weren't present at the conference or who just couldn't make this year, each conference offers a breakout session. . . .

The first day's breakouts were Lunch with a Physician. The guys adored their session. The girls. Well, maybe not so much. But day two, when we once again resumed those breakouts, there wasn't enough time in the day to talk, to laugh, to cry, to ask questions, and share stories.

For the guys and girls alike, topics spanned the social front. For the men, drinking came into focus, the should you/shouldn't you question. For the women, we talked a lot about fertility and family and what PSC meant for us in the traditional/societal sense of being a woman and in the physical sense as to what may or may not be possible given our PSC.

But both the 20s/30s men and women found themselves in similar circumstances as we discussed dating and how to tell someone and when to tell someone you have PSC. We talked about how fatigue affects work and friendships and, to some extent, self-esteem. We talked about medications and treatments we've tried. We talked and we talked and we talked. . . .

We asked questions of the 20s/30s siblings and caregivers who joined us. We mined their souls for clues as to how the "healthy" see us, to know what our diseases do to our loved ones and how we can help them or thank them for helping us. We talked as though there wasn't a tomorrow coming because our tomorrows will come but we won't be together. We'll go back to being the sick man or woman in the room. . . .

See, for some, PSC might stand for Primary Sclerosing Cholangitis. For us, those of us in this wonderfully wacky, extensively varied and lovely and large family,

PSC stands for Please Stay Close. . . . For we are together in the fight, whatever it takes.

And to those of you who became a part of my PSC family this year or who came and renewed the bonds, I can't thank you enough for strengthening me and for allowing me to give to you.

And for those of you who haven't yet become a part of this fabulous family that no one wanted to be a part of and now couldn't dream of being without, well, we're waiting for you. We'll set an extra chair at the table and keep all the good stories humming. . .

In 2010, Sandi and her sister Karen did a "meme." As Sandi described it, a meme is associated with Invisible Illness Week (IIW), held in September. A meme asks people "with chronic illnesses to open up and bare their souls and share with the world [by answering 30 questions] what it's like to be invisible and ailing."

Meme x 2[12]

Discussing the meme, Sandi said, "I've done it and it's cathartic and nerve-wracking and freeing and depressing and about 100 other adjectives. But something's always bothered me: Why is it only for those diagnosed with a chronic illness? Who knows better than a PSCer that while the disease may lie in our particular bodies, it's a community diagnosis? PSC affects our friends and families and spouses and siblings and it just doesn't seem fair that there's no meme for them."

Sandi's sister Karen agreed to do her own meme, and Sandi encouraged others to do the same. Below are some of Sandi's and Karen's responses. These responses provide a snapshot of how two people viewed the disease, from both its negative and, strangely enough, from its "positive" aspects.

From Sandi: 30 Things About My Invisible Illness You May Not Know: Some Time in The Life of a PSCer

1. The illness I live with is: Primary Sclerosing Cholangitis (PSC) as well as Ulcerative Colitis, Gastroparesis and more.

2. I was diagnosed with it in the year: Honestly, I don't even know anymore. I was so sick the whole thing is a blur. I'm guessing it was 2006 or 2007.

3. But I had symptoms since: I'd been sick off and on for years and one doctor after another told me it was just "stress.". . .

4. The biggest adjustment I've had to make is: Every single day with PSC is a million little battles fought in a (currently) unwinable war. I miss my privacy and independence. I miss my savings (being ill costs an awful lot). I miss my energy. I miss my cellphone being filled up with friends' names instead of doctors' names and nurse coordinators and transplant secretaries and pharmacies and the like. I

miss being able to count on my body and my brain to work the ways they always had in the past. . . .

9. The hardest part about nights are: Insomnia. I'm beyond exhausted so much of the time and I'm completely befuddled by the fact that my body won't let me sleep. I'm too exhausted to watch tv or talk or anything other than to stare into space and still sometimes sleep won't come! What's up with that? I don't need Mr. Sandman to bring me a dream, just a little restorative shuteye would be nice every once in a while. . . .

11. Regarding alternative treatments: I have tried so many of them. I'd say the one that works the best for me is mindfulness, trying to stay present and enjoying what life has to offer whether that's a great TV show, a conversation with a friend or even just laughing at my rascal of a cat. Part of mindfulness is also forgiving myself for things I didn't choose. So, I'm upset when my body won't let me do what I want, but I work on not dwelling there and instead I search for the good points to whatever the case may be. Oh, and chocolate sometimes helps a lot. :)....

13. Regarding working and career: I was devastated to lose my job when I became ill. Being in your 30s and unable to work is humiliating, difficult and hard to explain to people whose first question is generally, "What do you do?" I know my body isn't capable of what it once was and that regular "work" is not an option for me. But I still miss it (or aspects of it) almost every day! But as my friends and family tell me, I do still work. I might not get a paycheck, but the dividends are far greater. Fighting to eradicate PSC and being a part of PSC Partners fulfills my heart and soul in ways I consider myself truly blessed to experience! . . .

15. The hardest thing to accept about my new reality has been: that there's no normality. When most people wake up in the morning, they can expect their day to go a certain way to a certain degree. They expect to have the energy to get out of bed. They expect to be able to keep down their breakfast and remember the word for "car" or "phone." They expect that if they've made plans, even little ones like throwing the wash in the dryer, that they'll be able to accomplish those goals. For a PSCer, we can't count on any of those things. Despite our wants, our bodies sometimes just say no to things we need and want to do. In terms of doing the wash though, my best advice is to screw the laundry and just buy a lot of underwear. I'm a fan of Victoria's Secret myself, but your underwear is your choice. :)

16. Something I never thought I could do with my illness that I did was: Turn it into a positive. Don't get me wrong, there's PLENTY of suckage with PSC (hmm, I all of a sudden went Pauly Shore mid-90s on that one, huh?). Anyhow, PSC isn't fun and it isn't something I'd wish on even my worst enemy, well . . . :) PSC brings so many negatives it practically requires its own ZIP code, but it can also bring good. In my case, it brought closer, real friendships and focus on the

people, issues and things that really matter to me. It brought a realization that my life is mine to choose and I can wallow or laugh or sleep or play or see each day as a new possibility instead of one day closer to not having any more days, which, if you think about it, is a boat we're all in anyhow, might as well enjoy the ride and not drive yourself crazy scrambling for a paddle. . . .

19. It was really hard to have to give up: this idea that I am/was what I do. I had to learn to separate myself from a traditional job-titled society where you're measured by your paygrade and office size or the alphabet soup of letters behind your name. I'm actually still working on this one and I lost my ability to work and my job around 4 years ago now. (By the way, I don't mean to imply anything bad about people who are their work. Let's face it, whatever part of me isn't water and liver disease is entirely PSC Partners, it's just that I had to learn to separate and realize I can be more than just whatever my job title may be. . . .

22. My illness has taught me: Appreciation for what life has to offer. It's taught me to love with a bigger heart and listen on a grander scale. It's taught me that sometimes some of the most wonderful things in the world are born out of some of the most devastating.

23. Want to know a secret? One thing people say that gets under my skin is: Do I have to pick just one? I hate people telling me if I had accepted religion or religious figures properly I wouldn't be sick. I can't stand when somebody tells me they know a "surefire" cure (like rubbing sesame oil on my feet is really going to fix my PSC. Grr)! I'm annoyed when people offer advice and I thank them and then they still keep pressuring me every single time they see me. Okay, I'm really hung up on the sesame oil lady, but she drives me crazy! I'm horrified when people tell me I must have invited illness in. Why would anyone say such a thing? Oh, I also don't like it when people say the words "moist" or "ooze," but that's just because they sound nasty. :)

24. But I love it when people: remember I'm a person and not just a "sick chick." I love when people laugh with me and show me they care and ask questions because they want answers and not because they're trying to be polite. I love it when people surprise me with their generosity and understanding and I love it when people remember I'm not an only child and that my sister still exists and matters and that my parents are more than just the parents of a chronically ill daughter. I love it when people see me as a person first rather than a sick person and then, if at all, a person.

25. My favorite motto, scripture, quote that gets me through tough times is: Laugh, don't cry. Is that really narcissistic, to quote myself? It's what I live by though!

26. When someone is diagnosed I'd like to tell them: that they're not alone, they have a hand to hold and a shoulder to cry on and a partner in the millions of battles and wars PSC puts us through on a daily basis.

27. Something that has surprised me about living with an illness is: The irregularity of it all and the expense of it all. Also, the guilt can be a lot to take. All of the sudden, I went from independent to a burden (or potential burden, anyway). It's tough to reconcile all of that guilt. . . .

29. I'm involved with Invisible Illness Week because: everybody needs to know they're not invisible and that they matter. Because it's horrible to walk into a doctor's office and have them stare at you blankly and say they've never heard of your disease or give you unforgivably wrong information. Because it's our chance as PSCers to tell the real truth about what our lives are like and show others they're not alone and still others that we may be down occasionally, but we're definitely not out! . . .

From Karen: 30 Things About My Invisible Illness You May Not Know: Some Time in The Life of A PSCer. . . .

Upon hearing the diagnosis I felt: Scared, confused, but mostly ready to find out what PSC was and what could be done to fight it.

The biggest adjustment I've had to make is: Allowing for more understanding regarding how tired, sick, full of pain, etc., my sister is. I went from the bratty little sister to trying to be more of a support system.

Most people assume: That I grieve daily and I may. However, I do not think about PSC all day every day. In so many ways this disease has allowed a closer bond to form between my sister and me. It has allowed me to see her for the strong and inspiring person that she truly is. . . .

The hardest part about living with PSC is: Watching the toll it takes on my family. While there are positives I can see, it is hard to see the years it has added to my parents and the pain and suffering that my sister deals with on a daily basis.

I hope my PSCer knows: How inspired I am by her, all that she deals with and with such a positive attitude and, also, how she has become such a driving force among other PSCers to keep their spirits up and give them a place to vent and let them know they are not alone. . . .

One thing that surprised me about life with a PSCer is: How much more valuable a laughing fit can be or simply time spent together, although not necessarily the Victoria's Secret runs :)

PSC makes me feel: Angry, upset, bitter. However, PSCers make me feel inspired and amazed.

People would be surprised to know: That while I would never wish PSC on anyone, I can see quite a bit of beauty that this diagnosis has brought into our lives.

I'm embarrassed to admit: That at times I forget how sick my sister is and get annoyed by the fact that she cannot accomplish simple things. . . .

Something I really miss doing with my PSCer: Simple things like apple picking, walking around the neighborhood, going to events, seeing her in action in the library, etc. While we can still do these things, it is with much more difficulty for Sandi.

It was really hard to have to give up: That feeling that my sister was always going to be around, that sense of security. . . .

This illness has taught me: To appreciate everyone, namely my sister/family and just how strong people can be.

Want to know a secret? One thing people say that gets under my skin is: "How is Sandi doing?" I know this sounds terrible, but I get asked that question 20 times a day by the general public. While I love that so many people care, how lovely would it be if they followed that question up with, "What can I do to help?"

But I love it when people: Take the time to learn what PSC is, ask questions and care enough to get involved. . . .

When someone is diagnosed I'd like to tell them: You are not alone. And then I'd direct them to the FB site as well as strongly encourage them to come to the next conference. I look forward to the conference every year. Every PSCer and caregiver should have the experience of being in a room with so many others in a similar situation.

Something that has surprised me about living with an illness is: The positives that come with it. Granted, I'm not the one with the actual disease; but, as mentioned earlier, PSC has made me appreciate my sister and own healthy life even more and it's definitely brought my family even closer.

I know I'm appreciated when: I can make my family laugh. Laughter is one thing that this disease tries to diminish, but as Sandi always says, "You can laugh or cry. So, choose laugh.". . . .

PSCEer: the loved one of a PSCer. The E in PSCEer stands for either empathy or envy depending on the situation.

PART 3 – PROGRAMS

Sandi had the ability to see beyond, to visualize what was possible. For example, when she moved into her Fredericksburg house, she wanted to buy an Ikea wall unit that covered the length of one wall. I, her father, measured the length of the wall, not once but at least two times, and confidently assured her that the piece would not fit. She looked at me, at the piece, then at me, saying "It'll fit." She went on to buy the wall unit and to have it installed. It fit, with about 1/8" left on each side.

This same vision applied to many of Sandi's endeavors, including her involvement with PSC Partners Seeking a Cure. Sandi saw ways she believed that this relatively new, non-profit organization could be strengthened. And to their credit, Ricky Safer and other PSC Partners decision makers gave Sandi what I call the permission to fly, to try new things. And "fly" Sandi did. For example, she started a Facebook PSC support group that now has over 2,500 members, from many different countries; she started a mentoring program; she created PSC shirt designs; and in 2009 she started the PSC Save the Day fundraising program. She always was receptive to, and looking for new ideas. She loved talking with, exchanging information with, and being there for others. Sandi felt honored by the trust placed in her and strove to never violate that trust.

In this part, information is provided on several different programs begun by Sandi.

Save the Day

Save the Day was PSC Partners first ever fundraising weekend, October 2-4, 2009. In announcing the program Sandi spoke about our ability to become actively involved in the search for a cure. In the summer 2009 PSC Partners newsletter[13], Sandi wrote:

> Have you ever wanted to be a superhero, you know, rush in and save the day? Be the be all end all to countless men, women and children, swooping in and saving the lives of damsels (and dudemars) in distress?
>
> Well, now you're in luck because being a true superhero is even easier than ever these days and anyone can do it no matter how old, young, tired, itchy and/or sleep-deprived!
>
> So, grab your cape, boots and decoder ring and join us the first weekend in October for our first ever annual PSC Partners "Save the Day!"
>
> We all know that as things stand we're fighting an unstoppable villain. PSC storms in, takes over and there's little we can do to stop it. But every uber-villain thinks they're unstoppable and every superhero knows that the stopping is just a matter of time.
>
> So, PSC might have the upper hand at the moment, but with our team of heroes in the making, it frankly doesn't stand a chance. And when we band together, watch out world! October 2-4 kicks off our first ever Save the Day-athon. So hold those

fundraisers. Hit up those friends. Tell those villainous PSC genes they're going down!

On that weekend, the good guys are taking over. So, whether you're gathering up the funds from a year-long fundraiser or holding one for the first time this October, let's make this year's Save the Day one for the history books. Sound good? Great! Super! . . .

In her column Sandi goes on to identify some ways to "save the day" – for example, collecting donations through a spare change jar; a swear jar; community involvement; auctions; asking stores to donate 10% of one day's profits to the fight against PSC; letter-writing campaigns; and one's own creative ideas.

In 2010, Sandi wrote "**Save the Day: Dream a (not so little) Dream**"[14]

Do you all know the story of Rip Van Winkle, the dude who lay down to sleep and woke up some 20-100 years later (depending on the version you hear)? I've got to confess sometimes I envy old Rip. I don't want to be branded as lazy or be nagged and henpecked--and lord knows I'd hope somebody would be kind enough to put a waxer on retainer if I was going to sleep that long--but I do envy that extended blissful slumber that he got to take without a care in the world.

Then, we add to that the fact that he woke up years later to a world full of new possibilities and, wow, even the bluest of eyes might turn green. Can you imagine if that was our fate? If we could get some good quality sleep and wake up in a world where there was a cure for PSC? How amazing would that be? I mean, sure, there'd be a lot of drawbacks to missing the last 20 or so years, but we'll just suspend that reality for now, okay? :) . . .

Each October, PSC Partners sets its annual Save the Day international fundraiser into effect where we ask PSCers all over the world to step up and spread awareness and hold local fundraisers designed to let the world know we're here and that we're raising funds for a cure! The fantastic news is that we've got research grants just waiting to be funded and some of the most amazing scientific minds in the world ready and willing to delve into PSC and study the heck out of it. The even more fantastic news is that every single penny helps and FUNdraising can be done by anyone of any age. And, when we all do it together, all over the world, wow, what a difference we can make! . . . And if your energy doesn't permit you to hold your own fundraiser, garage sale, bake sale, etc. and your medical bills make donating even a few dollars impossible this year, know that we've got your back and that we know when you're once again at full speed, you'll have ours. . . .

Save the Day is an example of developing a program that can serve an on-going function. This event was designed for, and is intended to help us reach the place where families no longer lose a child, sibling, spouse, to this insidious disease. As Sandi wrote[14], "The thing is, unlike Rip [VanWinkle], there's probably not some magic folklore wizard to wave his or her wand and make things happen; so it's up to us to be our own magical beings and help to shape and create the future we want to be a part of. The good news is we can most definitely do it. . . ."

Save the Day was one vision that Sandi brought to life to win this battle - "together in the fight, whatever it takes."

Introduction - Mentor/Mentee, Newcomer Orientation and Facebook

13. . . . Less than ten years ago, I was worried about whether my boss liked me, if I looked fat in things and what strangers on the subway were thinking when they saw me (and why they felt it was okay to touch me in places even past loves hadn't ventured). I presumed my friends and confidantes would be there for me come what may and that nothing could shake those bonds of friendship.

Then, I got sick. I lost my job. Many of those "forever" friends wrote me off and haven't talked to me since, because of fear or lack of interest, I'll never know. I was feeling miserable, truly miserable and useless and like I didn't have a purpose in the world.[2]

Sandi used those words to describe what her life had become after getting sick and through the early stages of her PSC diagnosis. She had frequent nausea, no energy, and all the other "pleasantries" PSC and its complications can bring. Doctors were not clear what she had, but when she described her symptoms (e.g., liver pain) they told her that was not possible, and that perhaps she needed mental health treatment. The doctors did suspect cancer on numerous occasions, but outside of making everyone very anxiety ridden, there was seldom any clarity offered.

Sandi dedicated herself to ensuring that those with PSC and their caregivers were not alone, that systems were put in place for those who had PSC, and for their caregivers, to get, provide, and share information.

Mentor/Mentee Program and Newcomer Orientation

In 2009, Sandi agreed to chair PSC Partners new mentoring program. The mentors are previous conference attendees with a good idea of what past conferences were like. The mentoring program is intended to provide first-time conference attendees with information prior to the Conference and a friendly "face" in the crowd at the Conference. That's it in a nutshell, a reaching out so that those with PSC and their caregivers are not alone!

In 2011, this concept was extended even further, as two new activities were added to the PSC Partners Conference schedule – a "Newcomer Orientation" and a "Mentor/Mentee Casual Meet and Greet." The newcomer orientation was described as a way to "[g]et the scoop on who's who, an overview of the medical presentations you'll hear, learn about our dot ID system, what to wear, and ask the questions you might be reluctant to ask in front of the larger group. The whirlwind session will give you a chance to meet other first-timers and get a head start on a positive conference experience."[15]

If I may borrow from Sandi and her use of song, both of these programs were geared to help ensure *"you'll never walk alone."*

Facebook

Sandi and another PSCer started the PSC Partners Facebook page in 2008. As described in the fall 2008 issue of the Duct, ".... Get in touch with other PSC-ers your age to share concerns, ask questions and discuss what life is like when you're young and diagnosed with PSC. If you've ever needed a place to complain about the fact that you need to nap when all your friends want to do is go out and party, share how you deal with drinking, ask others about issues dealing with starting a family, etc., here's the place for you! . . ."[16]

The caption for this column showed significant foresight – "Attention all 20 and 30-Something PSCers (or those nearly in that range!). . ." Over the years, the PSC Partners Facebook support group has been there not only for those with PSC, but also for the caregivers, family members, and friends, for persons of all ages.

Sandi served as the Facebook support group program moderator from its initiation forward, at times having co-administrators. Prior to their both passing in 2013, Sandi's co-administrator was Philip Burke, who passed away in September 2013. In describing Philip, and what he meant to her, Sandi said: [17]

> There is a Philip Burke-shaped hole in the Universe. And I confess, I don't quite know how to get through the days and hours without him. Right now, I can't even seem to get through a two-hour stretch without dissolving into tears. He was my friend, my confidant, my protector, my brother, my co-moderator, my fellow PSCer and so much more. . . .
>
> I know many of you feel much the same way, that the world just isn't the same without Philip Burke in it. You're right. The world isn't ever going to be the same. But let's make it different in a way that would matter to Philip. Let's honor him by doing what we do best here, talking about PSC and all of its attending necessities and supporting each other throughout this journey. Let's raise our voices and talk about the need for organ donation. Let's raise research funds to help those scientists unlock every single piece of this puzzle. Let's band together and honor Philip and all those others we've lost, some far too recently and some far too long ago. Let's make a difference and let's be there for each other, because sometimes the best medicine in the world is having somebody who really, truly understands what we're going through by our sides.
>
> I'll miss Philip every single day for as long as I draw breath. It's not often one finds a friend like him. Having him in my life was a gift and I know that if there's a choir in Heaven, and that's where he is, that they're celebrating Philip and his voice and spirit. . . . I know you'll miss Philip, too, and please know that with each posting about your day or your health, whether posting up a picture of yourself living life to the fullest or asking a PSC question, you're not only making

a difference for other PSCers, you're honoring him. So thank you for being part of PSC Partners Facebook and thank you for the outpouring of support and sorrow you've shared, because it takes strength to say we're scared and feeling a bit less sure of the Universe. . . . And we'll know that with each posting, the subtext between the lines is love and respect for Philip and a desire to bring about an end to PSC.

Over the years, the PSC Partners Facebook Support Group page has grown, having over 2,200 members at the time of Sandi's passing in November 2013, and over 2,500 members as of this writing (October 2014). In addition, the group is international, having members from many different countries, for example, Canada, Great Britain, Sweden, Netherlands, South Africa, Israel, Australia, and Colombia.

The support group was established as an open group. The current language[18] states:

> This site is for all PSCers & their caregivers. Please respect everyone on the site. We may be different, but we're all in this together! As a reminder, this Facebook group is an open group. This means that the information you choose to share on this group may be publicly available to non-members of the group including friends, family, employers, prospective employers, insurance companies, and anyone else you would imagine that would be interested in your personal health care information. Please do not post anything that you would not be comfortable sharing publicly.
>
> We're thrilled you chose to join us here and to be a part of our group. It's our privilege to help provide information & education resources for PSCers & their caregivers worldwide. . . .

A few years ago, there was a desire on the part of some users for a second, more private group to be established. Sandi agreed to this, and thus established a "closed group" for those who would prefer this option. However, the open group continued, with Sandi offering the following thoughts on its benefits:[18]

> Every time I post here, I raise awareness of PSC not only by sharing my story here with those who have PSC, but also those who can read about it on my newsfeed, etc (which I've allowed via my privacy settings). I'm also making a statement saying that this is me and I will not let my illness control what I say and where, etc. I won't hide it no matter what or from whom. My choice isn't for everyone, but for me, that makes a difference, knowing I'm doing my part to get the word out there and to say I have this; it doesn't make me less; and to be very up front about PSC and what it has brought/taken, etc. There's absolutely no judgment for anyone who doesn't want to share that way because certainly many people might not, but for me, that's part of it.
>
> Another part is that more than a few PSC doctors and researchers have mentioned to me how much they learn from this group about what's going on with the PSC population, things they may not have realized were "bigger" than one or two

PSCers, etc. So, it's about that, too, letting the PSC researchers and doctors have access to what really concerns us.

Another very large piece for me is that I feel strongly (again, my opinion) that there shouldn't be a barrier to getting information, particularly with something as rare and still largely unheard of as PSC. Sometimes PSCers and caregivers need to lurk for a bit in order to feel comfortable enough to post or to jump in and feel comfortable sharing their stories, etc. And with this Open group, a PSCer or caregiver can find us, read what's going on with our community, access our Files tab with tons of great information, etc. and then join only when and if they're ready to post or when they're ready. Whether that takes them 3 hours, 3 days, 3 months or 3 years, it doesn't matter. The information is there for them when and how they need it. For the closed group, they'd first have to ask to join before they can see anything and sometimes getting and dealing with a diagnosis of PSC is all somebody can take and, even though it may sound silly, asking to join a group sight unseen, may just be too much to take on at any given moment.

And, last but not least, closed groups are still online groups, so I guess I don't figure one is "safer" than another in any way. Truthfully, no matter where we post, if somebody really wants our information they can get to it. For those who want to keep things out of their newsfeeds or have stricter privacy settings, etc., though, the closed group may be a really good option for at least some of their questions and posts.

Open or Closed group, both are run by PSC Partners Seeking a Cure and Philip and myself. We encourage everyone to participate in either or both PSC Partners groups and to post wherever and however often they choose. There really is no right or wrong. It's just all about preferences. . . .

Hope this makes sense! Whichever group feels or fits best, whether that's one or the other or both, we're just happy everyone is here and sharing and making each other's lives that much better by reminding us we're all in this together, no matter what. . . .

Facebook is another example of Sandi's desire and her efforts to ensure that those affected by primary sclerosing cholangitis are not alone. The support group is a first-hand example of the PSC Partners Seeking a Cure expression, "together in the fight, whatever it takes!"

The PSC Partners Facebook support group has become a setting where members can share their news, both good and bad; can ask questions knowing that in all likelihood someone reading the post has knowledge of, and/or information/experience on that topic; and can otherwise benefit in a largely caring and non-judgmental environment. For those desiring complete anonymity, Sandi established the practice of receiving those inquiries and posting for that person.

The success of the Facebook PSC support group can be seen in posted comments where group members express their appreciation for the group, saying that it offers the opportunity for members to share their thoughts and concerns and, in return, to receive support and understanding from people who "get it."

PART 4 – LISTS

Most of us like lists, both making and reading. Here we have Sandi's contribution, with her writings on a "Happiness Plan" and on "The Top Ten Reasons to Attend the 2010 PSC Partners Conference."

Sandi often said she had PSC, but that PSC did not have her. Her happiness plan clearly shows her thoughts on how a person can live his or her life, and to not have it controlled by PSC.

The Happiness Plan[19]

By now, even the man in the moon knows my mantra of "If it's got to be laugh or cry, pick laugh," and he's even getting ready to tell me to shut the, ahem, heck up as I repeat it to myself maniacally in doctor's offices, waiting rooms, at the supermarket, basically whenever life hands me a problem that I just don't feel equipped to handle, you know, like waking up.

Sure, some might consider it a personality disorder at this point, but I prefer to think of it much more like Ally McBeal's dancing baby or internal theme song, a reminder of something that I want that's eventually going to be within my reach. (And, yes, I'm fully aware that many of you are too young to remember Ally. . . .) But I think internal theme songs and stupid sitcoms and rocking out with your hairbrush in bed (or the hallway a la Tom Cruise--yeah, I'm old, check out *Risky Business*) are the things that make life more livable. PSC has taken so much control of so many of our lives. I think it's time we take some power back. I think we should make a group pledge.

Place your hand(s) over your hearts. I'll wait. I see you there in the papasan: hands up! This is important. Repeat after me, "I vow to do one thing every single day to make myself ridiculously happy." There was that so hard? And for those of you with roommates, spouses, children or animals who are now looking at you like you're a nutter, admit it, looking at their confused faces is sort of enjoyable, right?

So, how do we get to this great beacon of happiness on the days where PSC has positively screwed cheer? It's not that hard or complicated. Think about it, what makes you giggle? Feel beautiful or handsome or hot? What makes you forget, even for a second, about your PSC and upcoming colonoscopies and itching and RUQ pain?

Well, for me, that's largely anesthesia (which I am completely in love with. You know how some women fantasize about marrying doctors or lawyers or cowboys? I think my fantasy involves an anesthesiologist who quite literally can take me away from all of this madness. But I guess that's between me and my therapist, right?) Anyhow, here are some tried and true happiness guaranteed suggestions. Find one you like. Steal it. Wanna try one on? Borrow it. Have one of your own. Go for it!

Guaranteed Happiness Plan # 1:

On days when fatigue won't let you get out of bed, give in. Make a day of it. Every once in a bit, let the fatigue monster win, but on your terms. Cuddle up under a generous comforter (there's a reason they're called that) and watch some bad TV or pop your favorite DVD into the laptop or player. . . .

I have a guy friend who denies it but ALWAYS cries at the ends of *Rent* and *Titanic*. *Marley and Me* and *Steel Magnolias* are good choices too. Want to laugh? Try S*ome Like it Hot* or *Bringing Up Baby* or *Elf*. Fill in the blanks. You know you have a movie that makes you smile from ear to ear and, if you don't, might I suggest just about anything with Haley Mills?

In any case, commit yourself to the plan. It's not fatigue's or your body's choice to lie in bed all day. It's yours. You're in control and if you want to sneak a bit of ice cream or popcorn in there with you, who's going to know? And for those of you with kids or a hubby, make it an event. Bring them on in and introduce the kiddos to Mary Poppins or *The Wizard of Oz* or watch old family movies. . . .

Guaranteed Happiness Plan # 2:

Next time you're out and about, buy yourself a coloring book of your choice and the good pack of crayons. You know which ones I'm talking about, the yellow and green box that has the sharpener built into the back. Now, before you stop reading and decide that lack of sleep and medication have made me a loon, think about it. There's a reason why therapists use coloring as a tool to help kids work through issues.

First, it's hard to be angry or stressed or overwhelmed while you're coloring. Second, if you are any of those things, chances are that focusing on your coloring will help you sort out the issues that are bugging you or give you a safe place to vent rage: coloring Mickey Mouse a moldy green color or making Prince Charming have buck teeth can be strangely soothing.

Guaranteed Happiness Plan # 3:

. . . . Start a happiness journal. Write down three things every single day that made you happy. I don't care if it's making a traffic light on your way to work that you usually miss, a really good Bacon, Egg and Cheese Biscuit at the local fast food place, or that your dishwasher magically unloaded itself. Whatever the reason, write it down.

I've had days where I've written down this list: (1) Didn't throw up for three hours. (2) Cat purred and gave me a kiss. (3) New episode of T*he Biggest Loser* was on tonight. As you can see, it doesn't have to be earth-shattering stuff. But here's the kicker. One, I love my little happiness journal. It's brown and has a fabric fastener and looks like something Hemmingway would've had. Two, just making myself sit down at the end of the day (or continue laying down but with a pen in my hand this time) and thinking of and writing down three things that made me happy that day makes me feel like a nerd, but a happy one. And three, remember how we talked about the days when you need a good laugh, try rereading your journal. I guarantee it'll make you smile. . . .

Guaranteed Happiness Plan # 4:

Be honest with yourself and others. So many young PSCers I talk to want to hide their PSC away like it's a secret shame. I get that. I really do. It's such a hard thing to tell somebody or to make them understand. We want to protect those around us. We don't want to be a burden. Plus, to tell our truth, we have to think of timing and be ready for the risk of rejection and be willing to open ourselves up for judgement on something that is so much bigger than a secret stash of girlie magazines or bridal porn (which is what those of us in the industry call all of those bridal mags).

The only problem is that by hiding what is and what will always be such a large part of ourselves, we're perpetuating a myth that we're flawed and unlovable. We're telling others by our very evasiveness that we expect them to judge us and find us lacking. It's hard to bite the bullet. You might lose people who you thought were your friends. But in the end, instead of carrying around a bucket of evasions and creating a circle for yourself where there's no real support, you'll have ties that won't break.

You'll have truth instead of lies. You'll have compassion and understanding when you need it. There will be hands to hold in waiting rooms and people to celebrate real triumphs like improving LFTs and no longer looking like a banana after a fit of cholangitis and jaundice. In addition, what better way to advocate towards research and a cure than to be a walking billboard? If you don't advocate for yourself and make it known how important organ donation and funding are, who will? . . .

Guaranteed Happiness Plan # 5:

Spoil yourself. I know belts are tightening all around these days and not just from PSC weight loss. But I urge you to make the investment in yourself.

You can treat yourself to weekly or monthly pedicures (guys, trust me, if you're thinking this suggestion is too girly, you haven't experienced the loveliness of a pedicure for badly itching feet) or buy yourself a bottle of your favorite polish and do an at-home version.

Love to read? When you have the energy, hit your local library. I'm a former librarian and to me books are the be-all/end-all. But frequent hospitalizations and travel make lugging books back and forth a trial, so I'm thinking about succumbing to one of those e-readers and thinking of the expense as one for my emotional and physical sanity.

Grab a blanket and go for a picnic in the park with the kids and count stars or cloud-spot. Run through the sprinkler in the backyard. Stop by an animal shelter and take a lonely dog for a walk. Host a potluck if you're too tired to go out to dinner. . . . Get a massage. Color your hair. Whisk (or have your significant other whisk you) away on a romantic weekend in your own town. See a movie you've been dying to see. Designate a game night (can't go wrong with Clue, Monopoly or Scrabble in my book). Subscribe to your favorite magazine. Spend an entire day in bed watching Food TV. In short, it doesn't matter what you do, just make sure you do it and enjoy every second of it.

Guaranteed Happiness Plan # 6:

. . . . Log on to PSC Partners Facebook (. . . then search PSC Partners to find the group) and add what makes you deliriously, wickedly, convulsively happy. Then sit back, smile and know you've done a good deed for the day, you've made someone else smile.

The final writing in this part lists "The Top Ten Reasons to Attend the 2010 PSC Partners Conference." In this one column, Sandi sets forth the benefits she saw from attending an annual PSC Partners Seeking a Cure Conference. Although written in 2010, it is safe to say that Sandi felt these same benefits still applied in subsequent years.

The Top Ten* Reasons to Attend the 2010 PSC Partners Conference[2]

Everywhere I look lately, it's all about lists. There are books about making lists on the bestseller list (which further proves my point.) Commercials on TV remind me not to miss Dave's Top 10 list. Even the memo pad on my fridge begins with the words "Things to Do:" followed by a series of blank lines and numbers. So, although I usually dedicate this column to the worries, woes and triumphs of the 20s/30s set, I give in. I got the message. With no further ado, here it is: The PSCers (20s/30s) Top 10* Reasons to Attend a PSC Partners Conference.

1. Know you're not alone

So, the doc says, "Surprise, you have PSC. It's this rare, incurable..." and, well, there were probably more words but you were too stunned to hear them. . . .

Isolation is one of the worst parts of having a rare, chronic illness that even doctors have to ask you to repeat the name of, let alone your closest friends and family members. It can be incredibly hard to be the only one in a group with constant itching or the sound of sand running through an hourglass whooshing in your ear. Too many of us feel all alone and are stuck having to wonder if what we go through is normal. Do we know all the facts? Does our doctor know all the facts? What does PSC mean for my life and my future? One of the most amazing things about a PSC Partners Conference is finding out just how not all alone you are.

2. Experience the joy and hope

You'd think that a conference all about PSC would be at best heartbreaking and depressing and at worst invoke heretofore undiscovered suicidal tendencies. The truth is nothing could be further from the truth! Yes, it's a conference about a rare disease with which we all suffer. Experts go over the latest news in research and education. We hear some tough stuff. There are moments where tears are not out of line. However, mostly, those tears are running down your face from laughing so hard you start to worry about peeing [in] your pants again like when your best pal shot chocolate milk out of her nose in elementary school. Don't ask me how we manage it, but the three most prevalent things in any PSC Partners conference are joy, hope and laughter.

3. Become informed

The internet is full of scary "facts" as are, sadly, some physicians woefully unfamiliar with PSC. First and foremost, PSC is not a death sentence completely devoid of any hope. Not only will you hear from experts in different fields about the latest in PSC research, education and awareness, you'll actually be in a room with PSCers who are living happy, normal (or at least relatively normal) lives. You'll see firsthand that PSC doesn't mean Person Scared Constantly and that alone is worth the price of admission!

4. Be a part of the "in" crowd

In our daily lives, we're the other. We're the ones with the ticking time bomb in our livers, the need to go to bed before most 9 year olds we know, the ones who stutter when asked how we are and have to debate whether the question is sincere or merely perfunctory and wonder if the person asking could even handle the truth. At a PSC Partners conference though, we're the normal. Those caregivers and siblings and friends, they're the ones out of the ordinary. I mean, not taking a single medication? How odd! Eating without pondering what it means to their systems? Not having to know where the nearest bathroom is at all times? Completely peculiar! In fact, some of our caregiver attendees in the past have been so jealous that they're not at the popular kids' table, they've even coined themselves a phrase. We might be the PSCers, but they're the PSCEers*. A little sick (no pun intended), yes. Funny and kind of fab to be in the envied group even just for a bit...well, heck yeah!

5. Scratch, itch, nap in peace

Have you ever been sitting in a classroom or a meeting or a dinner party or anywhere and simply dying to scratch yourself...and I don't mean a quick ten-second thing, but a full-on make like a bear and rub against a tree to relive the itch kind of a thing? Well, at work you're bound to freak people out. In class, they'd definitely notice. At the movies, they're calling security and at a dinner party, well, let's just say nobody's going to be wanting to hug you goodnight or invite you back.

At a PSC Partners Conference though, you can itch and scratch and do so right out in the open without a single bit of self-consciousness. Embarrassed that you always seem to itch in non-public appropriate places (such as armpits, chest, um, God-given goodies), not only can you complain about it out loud, you'll find you're not the only one, and maybe even learn a covert method or two for scratching there without attracting notice. Caveat: Never ever do those things on a first date or a job interview if at all possible!

Need a nap to make it through a day? Want to go to bed at 7 p.m.? Well, go right ahead. No judgments here. In fact, we've long talked about the fact that pajamas as a daily-living requirement should be totally accepted (and not just by high-school cheerleaders). In fact, a pal and I even created a group for it: NAPS* Don't you sometimes think life would be so much less complicated if you were already in your jammies when the exhaustion hits?

6. Make lifelong friends

A PSCer pal of mine once told me that she feels that our conferences are like getting together with your very best friends--albeit the ones you might only get to actually see once a year. I can totally relate to that. There's no need to hide anything at these conferences. Seriously, you will NEVER find a more accepting group of people. Even things you're afraid to admit out loud to yourself are perfectly acceptable to bring up at the conference.

Not only will you most likely find that you're not the only one with whatever the particular issue is, but probably, you'll find commiseration and perhaps even some laughter and help to go along with it. Nothing is off limits for us. Want to discuss why your stools float, go for it. Want to complain that your gas or burps smell like rotten eggs, we've heard it before. Want to know if anyone else has to cut every single tag out of every piece of clothing they own just to get some itch relief? Well, I'll bet you dollars to donuts you find at least 30 people who are on board with that!

Further, bonds created at the conference last. We may not get to see each other physically very often since we come from, literally, all over the world, although occasionally just down the block as well, but we Skype. We chat and text. We FB. Our bonds are strengthened and lifelong. We can talk about PSC symptoms as easily as we talk about True Blood or our sad but unending love for Buffy the Vampire Slayer (despite having ended years ago) or Glee or how Thai food is so much better than Chinese. We can go for months without talking and still know 100% that our PSC pals love us and have our backs and vice versa. Where else can you walk into a room feeling perhaps a little uncomfortable or a lot nervous and be pretty darn assured that you'll come out with friends for life?

7. Get practical tips to improve your daily life

Got a question? Chances are, we've got an answer. Want to know if sweating or acne can be a part of PSC? (Unfortunately, yes.) Even better, want to know what other PSCers have tried and found either to work or not work? No problem, we're there to share. Think your medical team gave you bad advice? Ask if anyone else has heard the same thing and/or how they were able to talk to their doctors to make things better. Learn about different diets and lotions and medications and whatnot that make a daily difference in the lives of so many of us. Feel like you can't date or join your pals at a club because it's awkward to answer "what do you do" questions or be the only one not drinking? Wondering how others told their kids, bosses, pals, prospective life partners, etc., about PSC. Well, the answers are all just a conference away.

8. Find the meaning: Learn how to make a difference in your own life and other PSCers' lives if you so choose

Ever wonder "why me?" Want to know what you can do to further the cause? Want to find out how easy it is to hold a fundraiser to raise awareness and money towards a cure and better treatments? Want to have complete and total proof that you're not all alone in this? If you answered yes to even one of those questions, you guessed it, the conference is the place for you!

9. To be with people of your own age who like to, want to, or have to . . .

Well, you name it: Party, drink, date, be intimate/romantic, wonder about fertility, worry about what PSC means for procreation, figure out how to tell someone, wonder if children can be a part of their future, want to know when not telling crosses the line from privacy to deceit. Is taking a drink really endangering your life and liver with every sip? Can you drink wine but not beer? Is a little blue pill in your future? Can female PSCers get pregnant and carry to term? Can we still feel attractive and deserving of love and marriage? Are we lying if we don't tell our bosses what's going on or mention it on a job interview when asked if we have anything we'd like to say or what our weakest points are?

The point is you'll be in a room with people who worry and wonder about those same exact things. Instead of getting one view from one person, you can get 20 different views; you can find one that makes sense to you. You can have your fears allayed. And, well, for those of you who are single and looking, can I just say that we really are an extraordinarily attractive group of people!

10. **Put an actual face to all your FB friends**

Come on, admit it. You're really curious about some of your FB PSC pals. What better chance than this to actually check them out and see what they're really all about!

11. **To allow your parents or caretakers to talk with other people similarly situated so they don't keep asking you the same questions or saying "I don't understand" or look at you like you're nutso or seriously disturbed when you say you'd cut your own feet off to stop the itch?**

We all know it, the pitying look we get from our friends and loved ones (and sometimes complete strangers in the grocery line or church or wherever), that look that makes you want to scream. We try to describe what it's like to live with PSC to our friends and family but realize that they'll never be able to understand, even with the spoon theory.* I'm more than a little ashamed to say I've broken out into a full-blown tantrum when my father, thinking he's being helpful, asks me to rate my pain on a scale of 1 to 10. I know another PSCer who says he simply can't get a day free of his mother asking him if he pooped and what color it was and whether or not blood was present. I've also got to say that I feel enormous guilt at times about the stress and strain my illness has put on my family and friends. I worry they spend all their time worrying about and taking care of me and forget to replenish and spoil themselves. I'm scared they live in denial. I'm impatient when they don't know a medical term that's second nature to me (because we all know that PSC comes with a whole new vocabulary, free of charge).

The thing is I'll never know what it's like to be a caretaker of a PSCer, at least, I sure hope not. Our parents, sisters, brothers, lovers, pals, relatives, etc., are dealing with watching us go through something where they can't really tangibly help at the end of the day. They can't make our livers behave or our pain disappear. They can't stop the vomiting or help us think straight when encephalopathy sets in. They can't, much as they would like to, have our transplants and treatments and ERCPs and the like for us. They need to talk about this. They need somebody else to reach out and hold their hand and tell them they get it, and really, truly know that they each know what the other is going through.

It's not just the PSCer that is oftentimes isolated by the disease. It's all those who love us. The conference is a great gift to them to be able to find support and to hear the truth and experience the feeling of being in a room full of PSCers who are so much more focused on laughter, joy, friendship and hugging than death and dying. They need to be able to look into each other's eyes and cry and feel what they feel without worrying about putting too much on us. We need to give them that gift, not only for them, but for ourselves too.

12. To see who can make up the most memorable and useful phrases using only the letters "PSC"

Okay. I'll admit, this might not seem like a reason to come to a conference, but that's only because you don't understand how delightfully fun and distracting this game can be. Go on, give it a try...you know you're dying to give it a go! Here are some of my favorites from years past (some mine, some belonged to others...and those of you who they belonged to, sorry if I don't give you name credit..but I truly can't remember anymore at this point who said what.) . . . .

. . . Princesses Sleeping Contentedly, Please Send Cure, Pretty Suave Chicos, Please Send Chocolate, Pretty Scary Concentration, Patient Spending Club, Peas Sauerkraut Chicken--I'll admit this one makes no sense to me, but I love how if you say it with the right intonation it sorta sounds like a curse! :)

Anyhow, you all get the idea. . .

13. To better realize that having PSC does not mean that your life is over, but instead offers you the opportunity to explore alternative choices

Less than ten years ago, I'd have never guessed that I'd be living a life where I'd be listed as permanently disabled and be unable to work, where driving a car is only a distant memory and that I would have my own shelf in my local pharmacy. . . .

Then, I got sick. I lost my job. . . . I was feeling miserable, truly miserable and useless and like I didn't have a purpose in the world.

Basically, I was counting breaths until it was time to die. I wasn't actively pursuing death, mind you, just figuring it was quick on its way thanks to the ruins of all the things I thought I might have become.

These days, I get accused of thinking the glass is so full that it's slopping over the sides and that it's the size of a 10-gallon rain barrel. Polyanna* has nothing on me. It's not that I don't get down or blue, er, yellow, I guess is more accurate for us. It's that I'm able to see the forest for the trees. And I'm guessing you'll think this is cliched, but want to know why I'm largely sunshine and pink tulips? You guessed it, I went to a PSC Partners conference. . . .

I was part of something. I am a part of the PSC family. I'm part of an organization whose sole purpose is to have nothing left to fight for. We won't quit until we've cured PSC and made sure no PSCer ever feels isolated and alone again unless they so choose. We'll fight together, whatever it takes until the need for us is absolutely obsolete. . . .

Footnotes:

*Per Sandi's Count: a system where the actual mathematical equivalent is irrelevant to the amount of words and topic headings posted.

* PSCE: A made-up condition for the well-meaning friends and family of PSCers. PSCE can either stand for Primary Sclerosing Cholangitis Envy or Primary Sclerosing Cholangitis Empathy. (Ex: A PSCEr will claim PSCE when exhausted and needing a nap or whenever they itch.)

*NAPS: National Association of Pajamaniacs, a ridiculous group started just for fun and to spread my mission that Thanksgiving should be a pajamas-required holiday. Come on, think about it, it really does make absolutely perfect sense, right? . . .

*The Spoon Theory: a practical and easy to understand description of some of what life is like for the chronically ill [http://www.butyoudontlooksick.com/articles/written-by-christine/the-spoon-theory/]

*Polyanna: A movie starring Haley Mills (if you don't know who she is, don't tell me, it'll break my heart! Oh, and go rent the original Parent Trap immediately!) as a young girl who is exceedingly optimistic no matter what's going on around her. . . .

PART 5 – ODDS'N'ENDS

In going through Sandi's papers following her passing, I found a 2009 writing on Spirituality. In this, Sandi separated spirituality from religion, saying that spirituality is "…anything and everything that makes you feel connected and a bit freer from the everyday stressors of your world."

Spirituality[20]

We've all had them, days where we're sure we'd rather wake up dead or where even the tiniest inconvenience leads to a big explosion, maybe it's that you're too tired to finish that load of laundry, that you're itching so much that a severe case of poison oak sounds like a vacation or you're just plain old ticked waiting for biopsy results to come back. Whatever the trigger, PSC and stress go hand in hand like peanut butter and jelly on a third date. So, what are your options other than pulling out your hair, yelling at your loved ones or crying buckets? Well, there's medication, there's violence (which I don't recommend) and then there's spirituality. Now for some of you, spirituality is a hot button word. You don't want talk about religion or sitting around in heated caves in the middle of the woods while you expose your "information" to the bunnies and the bats. Not to worry, spirituality is something different for every person I've ever met and that's the good news. The better news is that it offers HUGE relief in busting stress..and that should have you unclenching those jaws and headed towards easy breathing.

So, what is spirituality then? Well, it's anything and everything that makes you feel connected and a bit freer from the everyday stressors of your world. . . . So, if it's sitting by a stream, dunking your toes in a pool, practicing yoga, petting your cat or a good long hug that lowers your blood pressure and takes your mind or your body to a serene place, go for it. Don't be ashamed of a good long cry (spirituality sometimes requires tears), feel free to ask for a hug. Define spirituality your way. Read a book. Take a bubble bath. Write down three things every single day that made your world a better place even if it's something as simple as "the sink is free of dirty dishes." Revel in what brings you joy and don't feel ashamed or judged. . . . So, start today. Turn off your phones, yes, all of them. Grab your hubby or your bubble bath or your dog and give spirituality a try. It's not just for organized religion or those who can bend their bodies in ways that would make a pretzel jealous. It's for you. It's for me. With PSC pleasure doesn't often figure in, so why not create some where you can? Make PSC stand for Pressure-free, Spirituality, Contentment at least for a few hours a week. After all, what do you have to lose?

Family and Laughter

Primary sclerosing cholangitis is an insidious disease. There is no effective treatment nor is there a cure (yet). On its face, this is a recipe for depression, sadness, sorrow, etc. And while these certainly exist, PSC Partners Seeking a Cure conferences, and Sandi's writings show there is so much more - there is laughter, there are hugs, there is a loving family environment. "Come as strangers, leave as family" is one expression often heard. Another common sound is laughter. Below are a few additional examples of the "family" forming and the presence of laughter which are so important for effectively dealing with this disease.

Whether eating pizza, going up to The Incline or just hanging around in the lobby, our group is restorative, loving, loud (really loud) and so connected even strangers know upon seeing us that we're family. We share stories and secrets. Fears come out to see the light of day and we learn they're not quite so scary after all. We hold the hands of people whom two days ago we didn't even know but are now forever a part of our lives, inexplicably intertwined through this madness called PSC which only those touched by it can truly understand. We say we're PSCers and caregivers, but we're all caregivers. . . . And the camaraderie is evident, we miss each other, need each other, crave this world that restores us all in our sameness and our abilities to lose our inhibitions and just be. We scratch; we cry; we laugh; we vomit; we dance; we go through box after box of Kleenex and we love. Most of all, we love.[9]

My little sister--now not so little at 34, I realize--refers to the conferences as the best time she has all year. Another PSCer I know calls them her family reunions--with family she actually wants to see. And yet another PSCer has actually told his transplant team that they'd better make sure he's either transplanted before or after the conference because he's absolutely not missing one. The reason [PSC Partners] conferences inspire such loyalty and reverence is simple. Everyone is welcome, wanted and accepted. There's no need to pretend to be a 'healthy' person and try to take a bite of something when you're too nauseous to eat or to try and pretend anything else for that matter. You're in a room where everyone is gathered together for the same thing, to become better informed about this disease that has brought us all to this place in time and to find a way to defeat it. We're not powerless. We're powerful. We don't need liquid courage or fortifying. We're enough. No matter how weak we sometimes feel in regular life, here, together, we're strong. . . .[7]

We stay up until 3 and 4 in the morning, so hungry for each other's company, warmth and presence that sleep, which is at once our best friend and worst enemy, ceases to matter. Are we itching? Sure. Are we scratching? Sure. Taking throw-up breaks in the bathroom and occasionally forgetting what we're saying as the words come out of our mouth? You got it. Do we care? Not even a bit. We've got gum, empathy and a quick capacity for laughter that drowns out even the toughest of nausea or deeply entrenched RUQ pain. . . .[3]

Together, we can make magic. We can raise funds and find cures and collapse and cry and laugh and hug and empower ourselves to make a difference, because now we know we're not only fighting for ourselves but for our family, our other selves from all over the globe who come together at least once a year to take a stand against the stigma of being the sick one, to forge friendships that stand the test of time and to realize that, like every fairy tale story I've ever heard, true love lets you slay the dragons, conquer the biggest of obstacles, and gives you wings to soar.[5]

Facebook Threads

We previously discussed the start of the PSC Facebook Support group. One area not mentioned however is the use of "threads" on a variety of medical, legal and other issues relating to those with PSC and their caregivers. The threads are clearly identifiable and accessible, even years later. New threads can be added. Examples of existing threads include "Stress and PSC – Share How You Deal with the Challenges of PSC;" "Asking for Help;" "Where Are You From" (to allow PSCers from given areas to become aware of one another); "Quality of Life;" "Registry Instructions" (to enter information on a database that approved researchers can access); "Dating & Relationships;" "Parenting when you have PSC;" and "Questions to Ask When Newly Diagnosed."

An unusual, but valuable thread is "I so hate it when... (because we all need a place to laugh and vent!) :)." This thread identifies well-meaning but often disliked comments by family, friends and others that those with PSC can frequently hear. Some examples: you look good, you must be feeling better; when healthy people "share their knowledge" on how PSC may be treated/cured; and the comments or behavior of others that imply you are being lazy, when in actuality you are simply tired. In addition to the sharing of information and knowledge on a specific topic, the value of these threads is in helping those with PSC realize they are not alone, that others have had similar experiences, including difficulty in dealing with the well-meaning comments of others.

In one of her thread posts, Sandi expressed her continuing struggle to ensure that while she has PSC, it does not have her:

> I hate that PSC is so all-encompassing and overwhelming that it sometimes becomes all we can see. I hate that we have to be on guard so it doesn't rob us of hope and laughter and love. I hate that it scares our family and friends and sometimes even complete strangers.
>
> I love that it's up to me to change all that. I love that I can laugh in the face of PSC. I love that I can make it stand for anything I want, like Pearlman, Sandi Cure. I love that, like George Bailey in It's a Wonderful Life, I now know to search out the joy in life since I'm aware of what everyone in the world tries to forget, that we're only on this ride for a short time. I love that I get to change people's ideas and perceptions of what life as a chronically ill person looks like. I love that it's brought me to all of you.
>
> But since this is the hate topic heading...one more hate: I hate that heat makes itching worse..what I wouldn't give to spend a day outdoors without scratching my skin off or being too tired to carry on a conversation while lounging on a picnic blanket...guess I'll just have to focus on the positive..those tulips sure do look lovely outside my windows and there's just no way to have a bad day while staring at beautiful freshly bloomed tulips!

PSC Stands For...

Early on, Sandi and others began to look at the letters "PSC" – the shorthand way for saying primary sclerosing cholangitis - and felt that something more was needed. The challenge became one of identifying alternative descriptions for "PSC." In fact, this was reason number 12 in Sandi's "The Top 10 Reasons to Attend the 2010 PSC Partners Conference"[2]. To some extent, this "search" continues today.

Some examples: PSC stands for Pee Speed Champion; Princesses Sleeping Contentedly; Please Send Cure; Pretty Suave Chicos; Please Send Chocolate; Pretty Scary Concentration; Patient Spending Club; Peas Sauerkraut Chicken; Pretty Sexy Chicks; Pearlman, Sandi Cure; Pressure-free, Spirituality, Contentment; Please Stay Close; Power, Strength, Courage; and Person Scared Constantly.

A Song to Sing

As clearly shown in earlier sections, Sandi enjoyed using song titles in describing her primary sclerosing cholangitis and on the benefits of PSC Partners Seeking a Cure, including its annual conferences. In 2011, Sandi wrote the following verses:

A Few of My PSC Things (to the tune of *A Few of My Favorite Things*)[3]

Itching and scratching in inconvenient places. Being too tired to tie our shoelaces. Being driven mad by what a stray hair can bring. These are a few of my PSC things.

Yellowing skin, ERCPS and constant dehydration. Mercedes signs without the car payments. A medical vocabulary without the degree. This is some of what PSC brings.

Swollen legs and middles and daily medications. Problems with both diarrhea and constipation. Forgetting what words we're saying even as we sing. Always wondering what tomorrow will bring.

When the liver strikes.
When the bills sting.
When I'm feeling sad.
I simply remember my PSC Pals
and then I don't feel so bad.

PSCers of all shapes and all sizes. Having people here from so many different places. Knowing that together a cure we will bring. These are a few of my favorite things.

Laughter and sharing and tons of random hugging.
Nobody caring what body part you're scratching. Falling asleep anytime is a okay with me. Loving what PSC Partners can bring.

Research and proposals and always fundraising. Together awareness of PSC we are raising. Power, Strength, Courage is what we will sing. Today's efforts we hope a cure will soon bring.

When the liver strikes.
When the bills sting.
When I'm feeling sad.
I simply remember my PSC Pals and then I don't feel so bad.

PART 6 – THROUGH THE EYES OF OTHERS

Sandi believed in the power of one, and in the power of us. She was, and remains an inspiration to many on how to handle adversity and setbacks. Even in many of the worst times, Sandi continued to use humor and concern to show her love and compassion for others.

"We met Sandi for the first time in 2008 at our PSC Partners annual conference in Jacksonville. Our first impressions of Sandi quickly proved to be wrong. She appeared somber and sad, reluctant to step into an environment that was defined by disease. By the end of the first day, Sandi saw that she had entered into a special, truly magical family, to which both of us belong. At the end of the three days, little did we know, that, within a year, she would become the shining star of PSC Partners and the clear and compassionate voice of PSCers everywhere. PSC Partners changed her life, and Sandi definitely changed ours as well." (Remarks of Ricky Safer at the Sandi-bration, November 24, 2013.)

Tribute to Sandi[1]

Today, as we write about Sandi, we think of what *she* would want us to say about her. It would have to be a positive message that could help others. Help others, that was key to her being. Help others lovingly. The only way we could do justice to her unconditional, positive outlook on life, is to share with you the beautiful lessons, we, and her family at PSC Partners, learned from Sandi. Being the passionate educator she was, she taught us many life lessons. She wrote millions of loving and empowering messages and articles in a vibrant and beautiful language that was unique to her.

The first lesson we learned from Sandi was that everyone should have a title! Ours was honorary second moms. On November first, that sad day she left us, we learned something new from the outpouring of love that filled our online space. We realized that she had made many others feel as special as we felt. . . . Her heart was so big that she had space for all. . . . She gave titles to those she loved . . . Using the PSC letters, she introduced the 20 and 30 year-old women's group as *Pretty Sexy Chicks* to an audience doubled up in laughter. It was Sandi's way of saying, "Look, we may have PSC, but we will never let PSC have us, no matter what." . . .

The second lesson Sandi taught us was that "The sun will come up tomorrow." Wanting us to chant the tune of this song, Sandi wrote, "You can bet your bottom dollar on that, the sun WILL come up tomorrow, no wishing on a star needed. No matter what life throws at us, and we all know far too well that life can be a big, old bully at times, shining a light on each other and on ourselves really does make all the difference. We don't have to live in the shadows, victims of a dreaded disease." Those were Sandi's words, and she lived by them. . . . Out of nothing, she created fun and meaning. She opened new days. Every day became special: There were Donut Days, Cookie Days, Thanksgiving Apple-Turkey Days … and we all joined in the fun from every corner of the world.

The third lesson we learned from Sandi was that each of us has the power to change the world. Sandi's influence reached far. . . . She changed our world at PSC Partners. She described PSC Partners as, "my whole heart and soul (well, the parts that [my cat, my sister and my parents] don't occupy!)" She changed the world one day at a time and had the ability to transfer all her joy to each one of us.

The fourth lesson we learned from Sandi was that we should allow ourselves to be colorful and daring. And color was always present in her life. . . . Our office is strewn with Sandi objects, each with the specific purpose of making us smile. We smile at her Damn-It doll, at her hilarious Christmas ornaments, and best of all, we keep her love notes posted on our walls. . . . We miss all the giggly moments with her, but the giggling *will* continue, as she has taught us to giggle and always find an excuse to have fun.

Another lesson Sandi taught us was that humor saves the day. Especially dark humor. Sandi would turn any bad news she received into a big joke. In her presence, we witnessed how, even the most somber-faced, unsmiling doctor, would become jovial and exuberant in her company. Who else but Sandi could think of giving human powers to a not-so-beautiful liver and of turning it into a caped super-hero mascot we could all laugh at? . . .

She taught us that it was okay to be mischievous and disobedient once in a while. Sandi was scrupulously ethical, lived by the highest values, yet we all knew that it was always, "Life According to Sandi." Sandi never lived life like anyone else. If she believed a cause was important, nothing would stop her. For a little person, she had colossal determination. Her mischief was an expression of love and commitment and was always a way of breathing life and joy into our community. She was the sunny leader of our tiny mighty army. In her words, "I'm asking you to *follow the yellow brick road*--and no, that's not a jaundice joke--because at the end is something even better than Oz; it's a place where you find that you possess a heart, a brain and more courage than a den full of lions."

Sandi talked about the power of family love, be it her own family or her PSC family. Sandi's love and appreciation for her mom, her dad and her "little sister," as she called her beloved Karen, were endless. About family support, Sandi wrote, "You'll save me and I'll save you because, quite simply, that's what family does.". . .

"For us," wrote Sandi, "those of us in this wonderfully wacky, extensively varied, lovely and large family, PSC stands for Please Stay Close. As in, the bonds we made are not fleeting and we need each other come what may. For we are together in the fight, whatever it takes."

Sandi, we will find you in rainbows, in owls and in butterflies, in shades of pink and purple. As you told us, "Once you're open to the love and beauty in the world, love pours forth, even from unexpected sources." We miss you, Sandi Pearlman.

PART 7 – CLOSING COMMENTS

Sandi Pearlman once described her childhood as "pretty ordinary" with a love of animals, General Hospital, a stubborn streak, and a passion for reading and writing. Other than General Hospital, those same traits remained throughout her life. One trait she did not mention, although evident early on, was a deep concern and a caring about others.

In 2008, Sandi attended her first PSC Partners Seeking a Cure Conference. Beforehand, she had made it very clear she did not want to go, but by the time the conference ended, she was in the fight. While Sandi certainly had her moments of sadness over her condition and what she had lost, these were short-lived and behind closed doors, as she believed and practiced looking forward, to see what could be.

Sandi got awards - but they weren't what motivated her - Sandi was about helping - showing others that PSC is not a death sentence, that a person with PSC is not alone, that a person with PSC can live a fruitful life. She drew her strength not only from within but also from the support, education, friendship, inspiration and love she received from those with PSC, their caregivers and others involved in the fight.

Near the end of her life, Sandi said that she wasn't sure she had been helpful to others. I assured her that the facts were just the opposite. This is borne out by the many comments shared on Facebook following her passing on November 1, 2013. In their posts many people described Sandi as an inspiration, others spoke to the positive impact she had on their lives. In one particularly heartwarming post, "[Sandi] was a friend unlike any other…. Until I met her, I never knew that one person could provide so much love to others. No matter how difficult times were for her, she never hesitated to ask how I was…. Some might think that the world is slightly darker today; I don't think that…. She is a star that will shine for eternity through the people she touched. Her body may not have been able to go on any longer, but her spirit will always be with us…." (Joe Hatchett, Facebook post of November 1, 2013.)

Perhaps it is only fitting that Sandi should have the last word. On a national government health website, Sandi wrote[21]

> Who are you? . . . For those of us with chronic illness, invisible and visible, who are we? What do we do? What are we in a world that defines itself by what our bodies are able to do or not able to do every single day?
>
> I'm a million different things. I bet you are, too. But I have an illness, one that most people have never heard about; one that most doctors have never heard about. It's incurable, has no viable treatments, can strike anyone at any time; and, often, it's one that is invisible to the naked eye. I have Primary Sclerosing Cholangitis, PSC. It's a rare, incurable disease of the liver and bile ducts that changes the way I have to live my life every single day. I itch as though

somebody poured itching powder in my bloodstream and then shoved me into an endless pile of fire ants. I'm nauseous. I have pain every single day and my brain and body can no longer function the way they used to. My exhaustion is so pervasive that it's mental, physical and emotional. Even my skin color is different. . . . and, yet, to the casual observer, I may look healthy. I get dirty looks when I use my handicapped pass in parking lots even though often by the time I've gotten from the car to the front of the store I'm too tired to accomplish my task.

I'm no longer who I used to be. . . . But I'm a warrior. I'm a fighter and an educator. I'm unafraid to say I have PSC or to take the time to explain to a physician or a bystander what it is. I shout my differences in the name of education and awareness. I teach others not to judge by sight alone. I teach them to listen and help them to find compassion and to want to cure me, to cure those like me. I show those with my disease that they are not alone and that we're in this together. I'm not a victim. I'm a survivor. And if my disease takes me tomorrow, it will be on my terms and because I've taught what I've needed to teach and I've said what needed to be said. It will be because my body can no longer take being "other," finding itself inflicted with a disease that very few know and that its resources cannot fight off. It will be because my soul has more work to do than my tired physique can support. And yet, should that happen, I won't cease to exist. Who I was, what I did, those questions may still be asked. The answers? My answers? More researchers and doctors and civilians will know the name PSC and will realize there is a war to win than before I came. . . .

The journey continues.

Reference Cites
(The following pages have the full article, minus some material that no longer applies (e.g., contact information.)

1. Rachel Gomel's and Ricky Safer's Tribute to Sandi. The Duct, December 2013, pages 1-4.

2. The Top Ten* Reasons to Attend the 2010 PSC Partners Conference. The Duct, Spring 2010, Pages 13-19.

3. There's a Song in my Heart. The Duct, Summer 2011-I, pages 11-15.

4. Once More With Feeling: My Return Trip to the PSC Partners Seeking a Cure Conference. The Duct, Summer 2009, Part 1, pages 11-13.

5. The Conference: Magic, Family and Love. The Duct, Early Summer 2010, pages 21-22.

6. Sanity Street. The Duct, Winter 2011, pages 17-19.

7. Three Cheers for PSC Partners Conferences! The Duct, Winter, 2012, pages 9-10.

8. The Love Letter. The Duct, Summer 2012-I, pages 10-11.

9. To Conference or Not to Conference? The Duct, Summer 2013, pages 8-9.

10. It's All About the Nap. The Duct, Fall 2008, page 29.

11. The Glass Half Full. The Duct, Spring 2009, pages 25-26.

12. Meme x 2. The Duct, Fall 2010, pages 25-32.

13. Be a Hero or Heroine and Save the Day: PSC's First Ever Fundraising Weekend, October 2-4. The Duct, Summer 2009, pages 18-21.

14. Save the Day: Dream a (not so little) Dream. The Duct, Fall 2010, pages 16-18.

15. New This Year – Just For Conference First-Timers!!! The Duct, Winter 2011, page 17.

16. Attention all 20 and 30-Something PSCers (or those nearly in that range!) and Facebook Fans:. The Duct, Fall 2008, page 9.

17. Sandi Pearlman's Tribute to Philip Burke. Facebook, September 24, 2013 and The Duct, December 2013, pages 4-5.

18. PSC Partners Facebook Support Group Page, accessed October 9, 2014.

19. The Happiness Plan. The Duct, Fall 2009, pages 8-11.

20. Spirituality. June 2009.

21. Who are you? A Primary Sclerosing Cholangitis (PSC) Story – GRDR participant. https://grdr.ncats.nih.gov/index.php?option=com_content&view=article&id=77&Itemid=148

Tribute to Sandi
Rachel Gomel and Ricky Safer
The Duct, December 2013, pages 1-4

Our first impression of Sandi at the 2008 annual PSC Partners conference in Jacksonville was that of a quiet young woman who appeared reluctant to step into an environment that was defined by disease. At the end of the three days, little did we know that, within a year, she would become a shining star of PSC Partners and the voice of PSCers.

Today, as we write about Sandi, we think of what *she* would want us to say about her. It would have to be a positive message that could help others. Help others, that was key to her being. Help others lovingly. The only way we could do justice to her unconditional, positive outlook on life, is to share with you the beautiful lessons, we, and her family at PSC Partners, learned from Sandi. Being the passionate educator she was, she taught us many life lessons. She wrote millions of loving and empowering messages and articles in a vibrant and beautiful language that was unique to her.

The first lesson we learned from Sandi was that everyone should have a title! Ours was honorary second moms. On November first, that sad day she left us, we learned something new from the outpouring of love that filled our online space. We realized that she had made many others feel as special as we felt. Everyone Sandi helped and loved, believed she was their best friend, and, in turn, that they were hers. Her heart was so big that she had space for all. She had an honorary fiancé, an honorary brother, honorary sisters, an honorary grandfather, and so it went. She gave titles to those she loved - Rock Star was the name she gave her dear friend from Sweden. Using the PSC letters, she introduced the 20 and 30 year-old women's group as *Pretty Sexy Chicks* to an audience doubled up in laughter. It was Sandi's way of saying, "Look, we may have PSC, but we will never let PSC have us, no matter what." And so the titles came and stayed.

The second lesson Sandi taught us was that "The sun will come up tomorrow." Wanting us to chant the tune of this song, Sandi wrote, "You can bet your bottom dollar on that, the sun WILL come up tomorrow, no wishing on a star needed. No matter what life throws at us, and we all know far too well that life can be a big, old bully at times, shining a light on each other and on ourselves really does make all the difference. We don't have to live in the shadows, victims of a dreaded disease." Those were Sandi's words, and she lived by them. "There is a song in my heart," she wrote. There was always a song in her heart. Out of nothing, she created fun and meaning. She opened new days. Every day became special: There were Donut Days, Cookie Days, Thanksgiving Apple-Turkey Days … and we all joined in the fun from every corner of the world.

The third lesson we learned from Sandi was that each of us has the power to change the world. Sandi's influence reached far. On a national government health website, she wrote about how a single person can make a real difference, "I'm a warrior," she wrote. "I'm a fighter and an educator. I'm unafraid. I shout my differences in the name of education and awareness. I teach others not to judge by sight alone. I teach them to listen and help them to find compassion... I show [others] that they are not alone and that we're in this together. I'm not a victim. I'm a survivor. And if my disease takes me tomorrow, it will be *on my terms* and because I've taught what I've needed to teach and I've said what needed to be said." She changed our world at PSC Partners. She described PSC Partners as, "my whole heart and soul (well, the parts that [my cat, my sister and my parents] don't occupy!)" She changed the world one day at a time and had the ability to transfer all her joy to each one of us.

The fourth lesson we learned from Sandi was that we should allow ourselves to be colorful and daring. And color was always present in her life. The Excel sheets she sent to headquarters were color-coded bursts of well-matched pinks, purples, and greens that brought us much laughter and delight. Our office is strewn with Sandi objects, each with the specific purpose of making us smile. We smile at her Damn-It doll, at her hilarious Christmas ornaments, and best of all, we keep her love notes posted on our walls. She was Community Relations Chair at PSC Partners. She created and headed our Facebook group. She created beautiful fundraisers. She wrote for our newsletter. But that covered so little of what she did. She did *everything* and more. Among us, we called her, "Queen of Quite a Lot." We miss all the giggly moments with her, but the giggling *will* continue, as she has taught us to giggle and always find an excuse to have fun.

Another lesson Sandi taught us was that humor saves the day. Especially dark humor. Sandi would turn any bad news she received into a big joke. In her presence, we witnessed how, even the most somber-faced, unsmiling doctor, would become jovial and exuberant in her company. Who else but Sandi could think of giving human powers to a not-so-beautiful liver and of turning it into a caped super-hero mascot we could all laugh at? She created what has become a most successful annual fundraiser and called it Save The Day, her Super Liver mascot leading the way.

She taught us that it was okay to be mischievous and disobedient once in a while. Sandi was scrupulously ethical, lived by the highest values, yet we all knew that it was always, "Life According to Sandi." Sandi never lived life like anyone else. If she believed a cause was important, nothing would stop her. For a little person, she had colossal determination. Her mischief was an expression of love and commitment and was always a way of breathing life and joy into our community. She was the sunny leader of our tiny mighty army. In her words, "I'm asking you to *follow the yellow brick road*--and no, that's not a jaundice joke--because at the end is something even better than Oz; it's a place where you find that you possess a heart, a brain and more courage than a den full of lions."

Sandi talked about the power of family love, be it her own family or her PSC family. Sandi's love and appreciation for her mom, her dad and her "little sister," as she called her beloved Karen, were endless. About family support, Sandi wrote, "You'll save me and I'll save you because, quite simply, that's what family does." With her own family surrounding her with their constant love and care, Sandi could do what Sandi did best – spread that love to those around her. She wrote: "From me to you, thank you for being the wind beneath my wings and for teaching me and helping me to teach others that [we] can fly… There's a song in my heart and a bluebird on my shoulder…"

"For us," wrote Sandi, "those of us in this wonderfully wacky, extensively varied, lovely and large family, PSC stands for Please Stay Close. As in, the bonds we made are not fleeting and we need each other come what may. For we are together in the fight, whatever it takes."

Sandi, we will find you in rainbows, in owls and in butterflies, in shades of pink and purple. As you told us, "Once you're open to the love and beauty in the world, love pours forth, even from unexpected sources." We miss you, Sandi Pearlman.

The Top Ten* Reasons to Attend the 2010 PSC Partners Conference

Sandi Pearlman, The Duct, Spring 2010, pages 13-19

Everywhere I look lately, it's all about lists. There are books about making lists on the bestseller list (which further proves my point.) Commercials on TV remind me not to miss Dave's Top 10 list. Even the memo pad on my fridge begins with the words "Things to Do:" followed by a series of blank lines and numbers. So, although I usually dedicate this column to the worries, woes and triumphs of the 20s/30s set, I give in. I got the message. With no further ado, here it is: The PSCers (20s/30s) Top 10* Reasons to Attend a PSC Partners Conference.

1. Know you're not alone

So, the doc says, "Surprise, you have PSC. It's this rare, incurable..." and, well, there were probably more words but you were too stunned to hear them. Since that time, if you're lucky, you've met other PSCers, connected at PSC Partners support groups and attended some or all of our conferences. If you're not that lucky, good news is it's an easy change to make! Isolation is one of the worst parts of having a rare, chronic illness that even doctors have to ask you to repeat the name of, let alone your closest friends and family members. It can be incredibly hard to be the only one in a group with constant itching or the sound of sand running through an hourglass whooshing in your ear. Too many of us feel all alone and are stuck having to wonder if what we go through is normal. Do we know all the facts? Does our doctor know all the facts? What does PSC mean for my life and my future? One of the most amazing things about a PSC Partners Conference is finding out just how not all alone you are.

2. Experience the joy and hope

You'd think that a conference all about PSC would be at best heartbreaking and depressing and at worst invoke heretofore undiscovered suicidal tendencies. The truth is nothing could be further from the truth! Yes, it's a conference about a rare disease with which we all suffer. Experts go over the latest news in research and education. We hear some tough stuff. There are moments where tears are not out of line. However, mostly, those tears are running down your face from laughing so hard you start to worry about peeing [in] your pants again like when your best pal shot chocolate milk out of her nose in elementary school. Don't ask me how we manage it, but the three most prevalent things in any PSC Partners conference are joy, hope and laughter.

3. Become informed

The internet is full of scary "facts" as are, sadly, some physicians woefully unfamiliar with PSC. First and foremost, PSC is not a death sentence completely devoid of any hope. Not only will you hear from experts in different fields about the latest in PSC research, education and awareness, you'll actually be in a room with PSCers who are living happy, normal (or at least relatively normal) lives. You'll see firsthand that PSC doesn't mean Person Scared Constantly and that alone is worth the price of admission!

4. Be a part of the "in" crowd

In our daily lives, we're the other. We're the ones with the ticking time bomb in our livers, the need to go to bed before most 9 year olds we know, the ones who stutter when asked how we are and have to debate whether the question is sincere or merely perfunctory and wonder if the person asking could even handle the truth. At a PSC Partners conference though, we're the normal. Those caregivers and siblings and friends, they're the ones out of the ordinary. I mean, not taking a single medication? How odd! Eating without pondering what it means to their systems? Not having to know where the nearest bathroom is at all times? Completely peculiar! In fact, some of our caregiver attendees in the past have been so jealous that they're not at the popular kids' table, they've even coined themselves a phrase. We might be the PSCers, but they're the PSCEers*. A little sick (no pun intended), yes. Funny and kind of fab to be in the envied group even just for a bit...well, heck yeah!

5. Scratch, itch, nap in peace

Have you ever been sitting in a classroom or a meeting or a dinner party or anywhere and simply dying to scratch yourself...and I don't mean a quick ten-second thing, but a full-on make like a bear and rub against a tree to relive the itch kind of a thing? Well, at work you're bound to freak people out. In class, they'd definitely notice. At the movies, they're calling security and at a dinner party, well, let's just say nobody's going to be wanting to hug you goodnight or invite you back.

At a PSC conference though, you can itch and scratch and do so right out in the open without a single bit of self-consciousness. Embarrassed that you always seem to itch in non-public appropriate places (such as armpits, chest, um, God-given goodies), not only can you complain about it out loud, you'll find you're not the only one, and maybe even learn a covert method or two for scratching there without attracting notice. Caveat: Never ever do those things on a first date or a job interview if at all possible!

Need a nap to make it through a day? Want to go to bed at 7 p.m.? Well, go right ahead. No judgments here. In fact, we've long talked about the fact that pajamas as a daily-living requirement should be totally accepted (and not just by high-school cheerleaders). In fact, a pal and I even created a group for it: NAPS* Don't you sometimes think life would be so much less complicated if you were already in your jammies when the exhaustion hits?

6. Make lifelong friends

A PSCer pal of mine once told me that she feels that our conferences are like getting together with your very best friends--albeit the ones you might only get to actually see once a year. I can totally relate to that. There's no need to hide anything at these conferences. Seriously, you will

NEVER find a more accepting group of people. Even things you're afraid to admit out loud to yourself are perfectly acceptable to bring up at the conference.

Not only will you most likely find that you're not the only one with whatever the particular issue is, but probably, you'll find commiseration and perhaps even some laughter and help to go along with it. Nothing is off limits for us. Want to discuss why your stools float, go for it. Want to complain that your gas or burps smell like rotten eggs, we've heard it before. Want to know if anyone else has to cut every single tag out of every piece of clothing they own just to get some itch relief? Well, I'll bet you dollars to donuts you find at least 30 people who are on board with that!

Further, bonds created at the conference last. We may not get to see each other physically very often since we come from, literally, all over the world, although occasionally just down the block as well, but we Skype. We chat and text. We FB. Our bonds are strengthened and lifelong. We can talk about PSC symptoms as easily as we talk about True Blood or our sad but unending love for Buffy the Vampire Slayer (despite having ended years ago) or Glee or how Thai food is so much better than Chinese. We can go for months without talking and still know 100% that our PSC pals love us and have our backs and vice versa. Where else can you walk into a room feeling perhaps a little uncomfortable or a lot nervous and be pretty darn assured that you'll come out with friends for life?

7. Get practical tips to improve your daily life

Got a question? Chances are, we've got an answer. Want to know if sweating or acne can be a part of PSC? (Unfortunately, yes.) Even better, want to know what other PSCers have tried and found either to work or not work? No problem, we're there to share. Think your medical team gave you bad advice? Ask if anyone else has heard the same thing and/or how they were able to talk to their doctors to make things better. Learn about different diets and lotions and medications and whatnot that make a daily difference in the lives of so many of us. Feel like you can't date or join your pals at a club because it's awkward to answer "what do you do" questions or be the only one not drinking? Wondering how others told their kids, bosses, pals, prospective life partners, etc., about PSC. Well, the answers are all just a conference away.

8. Find the meaning: Learn how to make a difference in your own life and other PSCers' lives if you so choose

Ever wonder "why me?" Want to know what you can do to further the cause? Want to find out how easy it is to hold a fundraiser to raise awareness and money towards a cure and better treatments? Want to have complete and total proof that you're not all alone in this? If you answered yes to even one of those questions, you guessed it, the conference is the place for you!

9. To be with people of your own age who like to, want to, or have to . . .

Well, you name it: Party, drink, date, be intimate/romantic, wonder about fertility, worry about what PSC means for procreation, figure out how to tell someone, wonder if children can be a part of their future, want to know when not telling crosses the line from privacy to deceit. Is taking a drink really endangering your life and liver with every sip? Can you drink wine but not beer? Is a little blue pill in your future? Can female PSCers get pregnant and carry to term? Can we still feel attractive and deserving of love and marriage? Are we lying if we don't tell our bosses what's going on or mention it on a job interview when asked if we have anything we'd like to say or what our weakest points are?

The point is you'll be in a room with people who worry and wonder about those same exact things. Instead of getting one view from one person, you can get 20 different views; you can find one that makes sense to you. You can have your fears allayed. And, well, for those of you who are single and looking, can I just say that we really are an extraordinarily attractive group of people!

10. **Put an actual face to all your FB friends**

Come on, admit it. You're really curious about some of your FB PSC pals. What better chance than this to actually check them out and see what they're really all about!

11. **To allow your parents or caretakers to talk with other people similarly situated so they don't keep asking you the same questions or saying "I don't understand" or look at you like you're nutso or seriously disturbed when you say you'd cut your own feet off to stop the itch?**

We all know it, the pitying look we get from our friends and loved ones (and sometimes complete strangers in the grocery line or church or wherever), that look that makes you want to scream. We try to describe what it's like to live with PSC to our friends and family but realize that they'll never be able to understand, even with the spoon theory.* I'm more than a little ashamed to say I've broken out into a full-blown tantrum when my father, thinking he's being helpful, asks me to rate my pain on a scale of 1 to 10. I know another PSCer who says he simply can't get a day free of his mother asking him if he pooped and what color it was and whether or not blood was present. I've also got to say that I feel enormous guilt at times about the stress and strain my illness has put on my family and friends. I worry they spend all their time worrying about and taking care of me and forget to replenish and spoil themselves. I'm scared they live in denial. I'm impatient when they don't know a medical term that's second nature to me (because we all know that PSC comes with a whole new vocabulary, free of charge).

The thing is I'll never know what it's like to be a caretaker of a PSCer, at least, I sure hope not. Our parents, sisters, brothers, lovers, pals, relatives, etc., are dealing with watching us go through something where they can't really tangibly help at the end of the day. They can't make our livers behave or our pain disappear. They can't stop the vomiting or help us think straight when encephalopathy sets in. They can't, much as they would like to, have our transplants and treatments and ERCPs and the like for us. They need to talk about this. They need somebody else to reach out and hold their hand and tell them they get it, and really, truly know that they each know what the other is going through.

It's not just the PSCer that is oftentimes isolated by the disease. It's all those who love us. The conference is a great gift to them to be able to find support and to hear the truth and experience the feeling of being in a room full of PSCers who are so much more focused on laughter, joy, friendship and hugging than death and dying. They need to be able to look into each other's eyes and cry and feel what they feel without worrying about putting too much on us. We need to give them that gift, not only for them, but for ourselves too.

12. To see who can make up the most memorable and useful phrases using only the letters "PSC"

Okay. I'll admit, this might not seem like a reason to come to a conference, but that's only because you don't understand how delightfully fun and distracting this game can be. Go on, give it a try...you know you're dying to give it a go! Here are some of my favorites from years past (some mine, some belonged to others...and those of you who they belonged to, sorry if I don't give you name credit..but I truly can't remember anymore at this point who said what.)

Pee Speed Champion --this one was attributed to our own PSC Partners' President by one of the funniest and most fabulous ladies you all will ever meet who happened to be in a stall next to our fearless leader one conference afternoon. (Seriously, meeting … and Ricky and Don and the rest of the gang should count as a reason to attend the conference; you'll get it once you get to know them!).

In any case, the list continues: Princesses Sleeping Contentedly, Please Send Cure, Pretty Suave Chicos, Please Send Chocolate, Pretty Scary Concentration, Patient Spending Club, Peas Sauerkraut Chicken--I'll admit this one makes no sense to me, but I love how if you say it with the right intonation it sorta sounds like a curse! :)

Anyhow, you all get the idea. . .

13. To better realize that having PSC does not mean that your life is over, but instead offers you the opportunity to explore alternative choices

Less than ten years ago, I'd have never guessed that I'd be living a life where I'd be listed as permanently disabled and be unable to work, where driving a car is only a distant memory and that I would have my own shelf in my local pharmacy.

Less than ten years ago, I was worried about whether my boss liked me, if I looked fat in things and what strangers on the subway were thinking when they saw me (and why they felt it was okay to touch me in places even past loves hadn't ventured). I presumed my friends and confidantes would be there for me come what may and that nothing could shake those bonds of friendship.

Then, I got sick. I lost my job. Many of those "forever" friends wrote me off and haven't talked to me since, because of fear or lack of interest, I'll never know. I was feeling miserable, truly miserable and useless and like I didn't have a purpose in the world.

Basically, I was counting breaths until it was time to die. I wasn't actively pursuing death, mind you, just figuring it was quick on its way thanks to the ruins of all the things I thought I might have become.

These days, I get accused of thinking the glass is so full that it's slopping over the sides and that it's the size of a 10-gallon rain barrel. Polyanna* has nothing on me. It's not that I don't get down or blue, er, yellow, I guess is more accurate for us. It's that I'm able to see the forest for the trees. And I'm guessing you'll think this is cliched, but want to know why I'm largely sunshine and pink tulips? You guessed it, I went to a PSC Partners conference.

I'll tell you the truth. I didn't want to go. I couldn't stand the thought of being stuck in a room with a bunch of sick people and talking nonstop about feeling terrible and all the rest. I wanted to hide under the covers and cry. Instead, I got out of the car and ran into Ricky and Don Safer about one minute after I arrived. Ricky's the PSCer, but there she was practically sparkling with warmth and radiation and buzzing with energy. Don had a mischievous twinkle in his eye and a hug and a grin that made me instantly feel safe and part of a family. I was still wary, but less so.

As the weekend wore on, I realized that warmth and sharing and frivolity made the hard stuff easier to bear and by the end of my time there, I truly had made lifelong friends and found a new purpose to my heretofore meaningless days.

I was part of something. I am a part of the PSC family. I'm part of an organization whose sole purpose is to have nothing left to fight for. We won't quit until we've cured PSC and made sure no PSCer ever feels isolated and alone again unless they so choose. We'll fight together, whatever it takes until the need for us is absolutely obsolete.

I tell everyone that attending the conferences is a game changer in the best possible way. I can. I know it to be true. I know it'll be true for you, too.

Footnotes:

*Per Sandi's Count: a system where the actual mathematical equivalent is irrelevant to the amount of words and topic headings posted.

* PSCE: A made-up condition for the well-meaning friends and family of PSCers. PSCE can either stand for Primary Sclerosing Cholangitis Envy or Primary Sclerosing Cholangitis Empathy. (Ex: A PSCer will claim PSCE when exhausted and needing a nap or whenever they itch.)

*NAPS: National Association of Pajamaniacs, a ridiculous group started just for fun and to spread my mission that Thanksgiving should be a pajamas-required holiday. Come on, think about it, it really does make absolutely perfect sense, right? . . .

*The Spoon Theory: a practical and easy to understand description of some of what life is like for the chronically ill [http://www.butyoudontlooksick.com/articles/written-by-christine/the-spoon-theory/]

*Polyanna: A movie starring Haley Mills (if you don't know who she is, don't tell me, it'll break my heart! Oh, and go rent the original Parent Trap immediately!) as a young girl who is exceedingly optimistic no matter what's going on around her.

To register for this year's conference and join the fun, go to: . . We can't wait to see you there! :)

There's a Song in my Heart ❋

Sandi Pearlman, The Duct, Summer 2011-I, pages 11-15

Okay. I admit it. I'm a musical junkie. *Singing in the Rain, Thoroughly Modern Millie, Mama Mia, Rent*, I could go on and on and...well, okay, on. But before you write me off as some musical loving goonie, bear with me a bit because here's the thing: in a musical, there's escape from the world in a way that just isn't generally offered in real life. In musicals, when something terrible happens, as it often does, there are still songs to sing, hugs to share or catchy anthems to occupy us as the tears roll down our collective cheeks. Musicals aren't just movie experiences, they're visceral ones. Even decades after watching a film, hearing the first few bars of the score transports us back. It's kind of like our very own time machines *traveling across the universe* granting instant access to memories, emotions and experiences. Honestly, even you nonmusical enthusiasts must admit to occasionally finding yourself humming along to a theme song or two-- right? I mean, who among us hasn't been whisked away to *Bali Hai* or wondered exactly how to spell *Supercalifragilisticexpialidocious* at least once or twice a year? And although the conferences you see in movies (Rosie's sexy dance in *Bye, Bye, Birdie* anyone?) vary quite a bit from anything you'll find at a PSC Partners' conference--although this year we did include bull riding, so never say never--still, they put a song in my heart like I'm *singing in the rain*. So, going with that, ahem, theme, here are a few of my favorite things about PSC Partners conferences and the memories and realities they make:

You'll Never Walk Alone.

Diagnosis of a rare disease which most people--heck, most doctors--have never heard of is downright terrifying. Like *Thoroughly Modern Millie's* Mrs. Meers is forever saying, "Sad to be all alone in the world." And it is...only, we're not. Let me emphasize that. We are NOT all alone in the world and there's no place in the universe that is more proof positive of that than a PSC Partners conference. This past conference was our largest yet and a whopping 62 percent were first-time attendees. That's 62 percent of attendees who took a leap of faith that a conference covering a rare, currently incurable disease was going to be worth their time, effort and energy.

So many of us walking through the doors of our first conference feel as kicked about and alone as Little Orphan Annie. We've discovered we are PSCers in a non-PSC world and feel it's practically a given that it's going to be *a hard-knock life*. For many, information on their disease has been scarce or nonexistent and, for an alarming number, just downright wrong. So, if you entered your first conference feeling much more *I shall scream* than *I think I'm gonna like it here* or those feelings have kept you from attending, rest assured, you're not alone. But like any good musical, there's a silver lining to be found and attending the conference guarantees...

The sun'll come up tomorrow.

You can bet your bottom dollar on that, no wishing on a star needed. No matter what life throws at us, and we all know far too well that life can be a big, old bully at times, shining a light on each other and on ourselves really does make all the difference. We don't have to live in the shadows, vampire-like victims of a dreaded disease. PSC is hard. Conferences can be hard. This one was hard at times and the next one will likely be hard at times, too. We don't have a disease with simple answers or very many solutions. The temptation to drown in ourselves and our situations can be downright enticing and to say a conference saved me is at once true and far too pat. But I can tell you that the decision to attend, for me and for so many other PSCers I speak with, helps us *[get] out of bed on the right side*. And because of that, even when we're feeling lousy, it's still a pretty wonderful day.

I heard from several PSCers that initially they were none-too-happy about attending their first conference and terrified to say no to whomever told them about it all at the same time. In my case, like in most of yours, before my first conference I'd never met another PSCer. Honestly, I didn't even particularly want to meet another PSCer. I was symptomatic, a bit angry and unwilling to take a leap into *a whole new world*. I was pretty darn certain that if the sun was going to come up tomorrow, I'd probably be burned to a crisp instead of basking in its warm vitamin D bestowing glow. I'd never been a pessimist before, but I was well on my way. So, when I say that the conference is life-changing and the sun is shining, I know from where I speak. I'm not some talking head where the words have no meaning and I know that when others tell me how the conferences changed them, they're not just whistling Dixie either.

Before each conference, I end up with an inbox full of e-mails from worried PSCers. People are depressed and they're scared and they're not sure they're ready to face a room full of the very sickness that plagues them like monsters in a child's closet. I offer reassurance, but it takes attending a conference to get it. I can tell you until I'm blue in the face about the benefits, but until you experience them, it's just words. As many of you know, I wasn't feeling well at this year's conference and aside from the yellow that I couldn't hide, I tried to play it off as best I could. But I was busted. A new attendee called me out. She's the wife of a PSCer, a symptomatic PSCer at that, and they were scared. They are scared. And she took time out of her day to sit with me, bring me a cup of tea and ordered me to sit still. We didn't talk about the events of the day. We didn't even utter the words "biopsy" or "liver." We sat and sipped tea, content in each other's company, an understanding between us that even when things are rough, as it was for me, as it was for her and her spouse, that there's nothing so tough that we can't attack it together...even if our attack plan of the day is no more than *tea for two*.

The conference has been over for weeks now and yet, the connections are not. Some of our college-aged PSCers have already hooked up for movies or pizza, skyping late into the night bemoaning how much they need sleep and miss each other. Others have made meet-up plans or written to me to see how they can be more actively involved in the next conference or with PSC Partners. Despite the official conference weekend's end, we're still *together wherever we go...*

Somewhere Out There.

Because that's the thing, we are together no matter the distance. We don't need Doris Day singing *Que Sera Sera* or the confines of a certain city to maintain our newly formed and newly reinvigorated bonds because they're more than a fleeting fancy. They're not just yearbook promises to be BFFs 4-ever. In big things and small, fun and not so fun, we've got each other's backs, fronts, livers and lives and we're well aware of *what a beautiful morning* it is. A first-time attendee mentioned he was having his first procedure a week after the conference. You know what happened? He got cards and flowers and visits from PSCers who just two weeks beforehand he hadn't even met. There were names on some of his cards that he didn't even recognize without turning to the conference photos for some help. We're not just *people who need people*, we're PSCers who need each other and when we say *I'd do anything*, we mean it.

When I was stuck in the hospital over Thanksgiving, my favorite holiday, hundreds of my conference pals spent their time making apple turkeys and sending me pics by Facebook just to give me a smile. There are scores of stories, volumes and tomes that even *Marian the librarian* would have trouble keeping up with and cataloging. And here's one more: There's a little girl in Australia, a true *super trouper*. Every year she holds fundraisers and every day she uses her tiny little body and all of her far-too-precious energy to send words of love out over the internet and out into the universe. She's waiting for a transplant now and do you know what's waiting with her? Aside from all of our love and thoughts and prayers, she's got some flowers...and not just any flowers, but plush flowers that have seen quite a few of us through transplants and long hospital stays, flowers that have travelled the globe *spanning seasons of love* and proving, once again, that even geography can't keep us from being *one of us*. See, our Australian friend has never been to a conference, but her flowers have and we know someday soon she will have, too. Until then, we'll just hum the *Sisters* song and remind ourselves that sister, brother, mother, father, husband, wife or any other delineation, we're no longer searching for answers in the dark, hearing our own worst fears echoing back at us. There are answers. There are voices and experts and people who have been where you are and are going where you're headed. There's no *I can do anything you can do better*. There's no egos. Not in that room and not in our group. We have medical gods (for lack of a better term) and they cry with us and hold our hands and rededicate themselves to the fight, knowing *we need a hero* and they are, we all are, the proverbial girls who just *can't say no*. We're a team and there's strength in numbers. When we're together in that room, in each other's lives, we're not the other. We're not even the sick. We're the kids at the popular table who have the whole world shining upon us so bright that we practically need to wear shades. We can do anything. We're *free to be you and me* (see, the musical references just keep coming!). Normal rules don't apply. When we're together, we *come together* instead of sleeping the day away or even wanting to. We're announcing we get by...

With a Little Help From [our] Friends.

We stay up until 3 and 4 in the morning, so hungry for each other's company, warmth and presence that sleep, which is at once our best friend and worst enemy, ceases to matter. Are we itching? Sure. Are we scratching? Sure. Taking throw-up breaks in the bathroom and occasionally forgetting what we're saying as the words come out of our mouth? You got it. Do we care? Not even a bit. We've got gum, empathy and a quick capacity for laughter that drowns out even the toughest of nausea or deeply entrenched RUQ pain. High on pop (you girls know who you are!) or high on each other, we've formed bonds that outlast a few simple days. Whether connecting on Facebook or phone, in person or at a hospital, we refuse to simply say

Goodnight, Sweetheart when a conference must finally come to an all-too-soon end. It doesn't matter if we're discussing *So You Think You Can Dance* or CCA odds, transplant or our love for tiramisu, I don't have a day go by that I don't hear from a member of my PSC family. And that makes me an incredibly blessed girl. And it's not just me that's staying connected. So, I'm asking...

Take a Chance on Me.

I beg you. Not just me, but on you as well. *We are family*. So, *let's get together*, yeah? I know I'm asking a lot of some of you to put your faith in me and in PSC Partners. I'm asking you to *follow the yellow brick road*--and no, that's not a jaundice joke--because at the end is something even better than Oz; it's a place where you not only find that you possess a heart, a brain and more courage than a den full of lions. It's a place where in one weekend, a few short hours, you can change your life. It's so much more than *a spoonful of sugar* designed to mask the bitter and the tough. It's a place where you know you *must've done something good*. So whether you can get behind pulling down curtains to somehow garner enough fabric for 7 children's playclothes or simply can't fathom the thought that anybody would name their child *Truly Scrumptious*, just remember that for so many, for me, when our annual PSC Partners conference ends each year, it says so much more than *so long, farewell*. We might have tears in our eyes. We might have lumps in our throats. We might be more than a bit weepy about the thought of waking up tomorrow and not seeing the faces of those who love us, understand us and have become as much a part of our systems as our own breath over the course of the weekend. But we also are saying *Good Morning* to a whole new life, one in which there's definitely something to sing about.

So from me to you, thank you for being *the wind beneath my wings* and for teaching me and helping me to teach others that *[we] can fly*. Until next conference, there's a song in my heart and a bluebird on my shoulder...and if you don't know what that means, well, you've clearly got some musicals to watch....

* Wondering what musicals and movies were quoted in this article? Sounds like a perfect reason to Goodsearch (goodsearch.com) for PSC Partners! Oh, and if you're feeling a bit sing-songy yourself at the moment, give the song below a try [next page]...after all, we say, "*if you want to sing out, sing out.*" And if you're thinking singing out is where it's at and want to send us a videotape of you singing the blues away, you'd make our day! Send videos (for PSC Partners use only) to. . .

A Few of My PSC Things (to the tune of *A Few of My Favorite Things* - verses by Sandi Pearlman):

Itching and scratching in inconvenient places. Being too tired to tie our shoelaces. Being driven mad by what a stray hair can bring. These are a few of my PSC things.

Yellowing skin, ERCPS and constant dehydration. Mercedes signs without the car payments. A medical vocabulary without the degree. This is some of what PSC brings.

Swollen legs and middles and daily medications. Problems with both diarrhea and constipation. Forgetting what words we're saying even as we sing. Always wondering what tomorrow will bring.

When the liver strikes.
When the bills sting.
When I'm feeling sad.
I simply remember my PSC Pals
and then I don't feel so bad.

PScers of all shapes and all sizes. Having people here from so many different places. Knowing that together a cure we will bring. These are a few of my favorite things.

Laughter and sharing and tons of random hugging.
Nobody caring what body part you're scratching. Falling asleep anytime is a okay with me. Loving what PSC Partners can bring.

Research and proposals and always fundraising. Together awareness of PSC we are raising. Power, Strength, Courage is what we will sing. Today's efforts we hope a cure will soon bring.

When the liver strikes.
When the bills sting.
When I'm feeling sad.
I simply remember my PSC Pals and then I don't feel so bad.

Once More With Feeling: My Return Trip to the PSC Partners Seeking a Cure Conference
Sandi Pearlman, The Duct, Summer 2009, Part 1, pages 11-13

The thing I love about life-altering experiences is that even when you expect them, they can still turn out to surprise you with the myriad of ways they can touch your heart.

I mean, I knew my first PSC Partners Conference had made me into a much-improved person from the shell-shocked PSCer who walked through the doors that first Friday afternoon. I'd been given confidence, a purpose, friendships that have stood the tests of time and frequent hospitalizations.

So, when Chicago rolled around, for months on end I proudly stepped forward and touted the glories of the conference to every prospective attendee for as long and as loud as I could. I figured I knew, so to speak, what I was getting into, what would await others. I mean, I was no longer a first timer.

I already knew about the warmth of the attendees, the staggering intellect of the speakers and PSCers combined, the sheer breadth of topics covered and even a good number of the people I would see. My goal for this year's Chicago conference was to help make sure others got that life-changing experience and to sort of live it vicariously through them.

And then I arrived and realized that life changing isn't just once in a lifetime and it's not just for those who have never been a part of a PSC Partners Conference before.

To be honest, I'm not sure when it hit me. It may have been when the first attendees started wandering the halls. It may have been as we were packing up and preparing goody bags to hand out. It doesn't really matter. All that matters is that suddenly, I was at ease.

I felt relaxed and happy and whole. I wasn't the sick girl in the room. I wasn't the one people were whispering about with the rare incurable disease. I wasn't even the only one exhausted and scratching and itching and forgetting my words before they could come out of my mouth.

I was just in a room with a bunch of people like me who were proudly wearing their blue dots (PSCers) and their yellow dots (caregivers) and their red dots (first-timers) and green ones (transplant) all declaring that we were members of the same group, of the same family—that we were the ones who belonged.

The conference was filled with well-credentialed speakers and researchers. Some of the news was grim and some was grand. But for me, the magic of the experience was the sheer number of us.

It seemed no matter where in the room you looked, there was another 20/30 something. We were there. We were listening. We were in this together. For those of us who knew each other before, seeing each other again was like seeing a family member whose presence you'd missed without realizing it until you saw their face. Sort of like having a part of you filled in when you hadn't even realized you missed it.

One of my beautiful PSC pals said to me, you know, I feel like you're all my best friends who I can share everything and anything with, even though I only get to see you once a year or so. And she's right. Except I'd say that what we feel goes beyond friendship really, to sort of a more familial level.

There is such a safety in the room, in that group of individuals. There's no hiding of symptoms or exhaustion. There's no embarrassment or accusation. There's just overwhelming support and love and understanding. And the thing is, it isn't limited. It's not just blue dotters (PSCers) to blue dotters but also blue to red (first-timers) and blue to yellow (caregiver) or green (transplant) or whomever.

By the end of the first day, the dots didn't matter. We were a PSC family old and new and all together. We'd known each other a year, ten years, ten minutes. It didn't matter and it never would again.

Some of what we heard at the conference was rough. Some speakers hammered us over and over again with the fact that many of us might likely die before we'd ever get a cadaveric donor. Some spoke about trials that we'd had our hearts and minds invested in as though they were somewhat laughable.

And some validated us. One speaker in particular spoke of the exhaustion that pervades so many of our lives and told us that exhaustion is real, that we're not lazy. That exhaustion is mental, physical, emotional and pervasive. I know several 20s/30s who would have stood up and applauded at this, you know, had they not been so exhausted.

Another speaker spoke about SSDI and advocating for yourself and how FMLA can be your friend. At this, one 20/30 something pulled me aside and just said he felt as though he'd been given a new lease on life, that he actually saw that he wasn't alone, that there was help. What could be bigger than that? And while he didn't cry, I can tell you I came darn close to it!

But for most of us, no matter how fabulous the speakers are (and they are) or how many statistics and studies are named, the true healing and education comes not in the doctors' speeches or through the painstakingly made presentations. No, those educate. Those give us food for thought. But those aren't the true reason that the conference means what it does.

Quite simply, it's the togetherness. Whether through breakout groups or just hanging out in hotel lobbies, the real miracle of the conference for all of us, at least in the 20s/30s group, is each other.

For those of you who weren't present at the conference or who just couldn't make this year, each conference offers a breakout session. More than one, actually, but we'll leave that be for the moment. The 20s/30s breakouts were separated into 20s/30s males and 20s/30s females and while it broke my heart to leave all those handsome men in another room, those breakouts are breakthroughs.

The first day's breakouts were Lunch with a Physician. The guys adored their session. The girls. Well, maybe not so much. But day two, when we once again resumed those breakouts, there wasn't enough time in the day to talk, to laugh, to cry, to ask questions, and share stories.

For the guys and girls alike, topics spanned the social front. For the men, drinking came into focus, the should you/shouldn't you question. For the women, we talked a lot about fertility and family and what PSC meant for us in the traditional/societal sense of being a woman and in the physical sense as to what may or may not be possible given our PSC.

But both the 20s/30s men and women found themselves in similar circumstances as we discussed dating and how to tell someone and when to tell someone you have PSC. We talked about how fatigue affects work and friendships and, to some extent, self-esteem. We talked about medications and treatments we've tried. We talked and we talked and we talked. And had we not had to go back to the main room, who knows, we may have been talking still.

We asked questions of the 20s/30s siblings and caregivers who joined us. We mined their souls for clues as to how the "healthy" see us, to know what our diseases do to our loved ones and how we can help them or thank them for helping us. We talked as though there wasn't a tomorrow coming because our tomorrows will come but we won't be together. We'll go back to being the sick man or woman in the room.

Our blue dot status won't make us rock stars or one of the cool kids. It'll be life as we knew it...only, life a little better than before. Because, see, for the 20s/30s and, I'm willing to bet, the group at large, the magic moments of the conference have less to do with location and hotels and doctors pedigrees and more to do with depth of understanding and compassion and unity.

See, for some, PSC might stand for Primary Sclerosing Cholangitis. For us, those of us in this wonderfully wacky, extensively varied and lovely and large family, PSC stands for Please Stay Close. As in, the bonds we made are not fleeting and we need each other come what may. For we are together in the fight, whatever it takes.

And to those of you who became a part of my PSC family this year or who came and renewed the bonds, I can't thank you enough for strengthening me and for allowing me to give to you.

And for those of you who haven't yet become a part of this fabulous family that no one wanted to be a part of and now couldn't dream of being without, well, we're waiting for you. We'll set an extra chair at the table and keep all the good stories humming for when we see you in Hartford.

The Conference: Magic, Family and Love
Sandi Pearlman, The Duct, Early Summer 2010, pages 21-22

There's a song by The Lovin' Spoonful that starts, "Do you believe in Magic [....] How the music can free her, wherever it starts . . ." And regardless of your mood, you sort of find yourself humming along and a bit peppier when those opening chords strike no matter your age or disposition or even musical leanings. I mean, true, when it's stuck in your head and won't leave it's not quite so magical, but I digress.

In any case, I dare to say that The Lovin' Spoonful had never heard of PSC and I'm utterly positive that they've never attended a PSC Partners Conference, and, yet, their upbeat, infectious, grin-inducing song perfectly encapsulates the magnetic kind of magic that emerges as soon as you cross the threshold into conference territory and take in your very first PSCer.

It doesn't matter if you've been to every conference or never before; if you're feeling old and crusty and cranky, like you've traveled too far to a destination you're not sure you wanted to reach. You can be open to it or closed off, but it'll still get you. It's actually more than magic. It's love, the kind we all dream about, not the kind with heaving bosoms, ripping bodices and ridiculous code words for all types of anatomy, but the real, lasting, unadulterated somebody knows me at my core and really, truly gets me kind of love.

Those who have never been to a conference before may doubt me. I don't blame you. I'd doubt me too. In fact, every year as the next conference grows closer, I do doubt me.

I wonder if my glasses have gotten a bit rosy and I'm remembering the conference like that of a long lost love: perfect, without flaw and ultimately impossible to have been real, let alone recapture.

Then that magic hits. It's not about the location or hotel or even that moment of arrival when you get that high from knowing a bed (or a bathroom or a Starbucks or whatever) is near. It's a physical thing, a shifting of organisms in our souls so deftly that our outlook is forever changed. It's that feeling that you're no longer alone.

You're not an outsider. For a few sweet, all-too-short days, you're—we're—not the other. We don't have to explain anything because to be too tired to carry on a conversation or so itchy that you can't stop scratching is the status quo. There's no explanation that you're fatigued and what that means. We know. We get it.

Here's the thing: Conferences are kind of like Vegas and you know the whole "what happens in" motto by now, I'm sure—and if not, you need to watch a bit more TV.

In any case, I can tell you this: sitting in a room with your fellow PSCers is freeing in a way even the best illicit drugs can't compete with (or so I'd assume). The trip we take with and from each other has monumental highs and crushing lows but it never waivers in its connection.

Deepest fears and secret goals are voiced without alarm about judgments. Hearts break and heal a bit better than before many times over. We stick to the horror movie rules that there's strength in numbers and take comfort in the fact that we're no longer wandering down those dark, creaky basement steps alone.

You can read throughout the rest of this newsletter about all the activities, speakers, presentations and everything else that our conferences are known for. This isn't small stuff and I don't mean to make it sound that way. It's amazing and informative and every single year I attend the conference I come away with so much more knowledge than I possessed upon arrival and I'm a stronger PSCer and a more informed patient because of it. But as intoxicating as all of that is, it's not the true magic.

Here's what is: Suddenly, we're not PSCers with whispered tones. We're PSCers loud and proud and, quite frankly, the envy of many of the others in the room. We're the cool kids. We're the trendsetters and we're the norm. We relish our time together. We don't need words or labels or descriptions to understand. We just know.

Having PSC gives us a shorthand that defies the need for vocabulary. We're greedy for our time together. When the days' events end, we're still just beginning. It's when we're most free to put on our baggiest sweats and pull on our baseball caps and break out the ponytail holders and slippers. It's when we share the stories of our lives, the real details: we talk husbands, wives, lovers, friends, kiddos, pets, movies and all the rest; but we also talk pain, emotional and physical, and tell our medical stories, what led to diagnosis or a new medicine we've tried that works so well we actually get why we take it. Sometimes we cry, heaving sobs that require arms around the shoulders and a group hug.

Mostly though, we laugh. We talk and we listen. We gather in groups big and small and float in and out of conversations. We, who usually find ourselves ready for bed at 7 p.m. stay up until 1:00 or 2:00 in the morning just relishing the experiences of those who, like us, know what it's like to live our lives. By the end of the weekend, we're stronger. There's just no other way to put it.

We're stronger physically and emotionally. Our bonds are renewed and our faith in ourselves restored.

Some of us talk. We get it all out where we know we're safe and loved and our words are strong and taken in and kept close to everyone's hearts and confidences. But it's not even about being able to say the words yourself.

There are those of us who are still afraid to speak, too newly diagnosed to voice our deepest fears and, yet, when somebody else does it's the most heartbreaking, beautiful, freeing kind of pain you can imagine. Suddenly, something that preys on you, makes monsters out of the shadows in your mind is vanquished. No matter the fear, chances are another PSCer has it, has had it, or understands it.

Here, in the confines of the conference, of our newfound family, secrets are safe and fears hold no power. Alone, we're afraid, but together we're strong.

Together, we can make magic. We can raise funds and find cures and collapse and cry and laugh and hug and empower ourselves to make a difference, because now we know we're not only fighting for ourselves but for our family, our other selves from all over the globe who come together at least once a year to take a stand against the stigma of being the sick one, to forge friendships that stand the test of time and to realize that, like every fairy tale story I've ever heard, true love lets you slay the dragons, conquer the biggest of obstacles, and gives you wings to soar.

Sanity Street

Sandi Pearlman, The Duct, Winter 2011, pages 17-19

Do you remember the opening song to Sesame Street? It goes something like this: "Sunny day, sweepin' the clouds away. On my way to where the air is sweet."

I mean, sure, in the case of the song it's all about how to get to Sesame Street. But I think we can co-opt it a bit and substitute "Sanity Street" instead.

Because the lyrics to the song are so fitting it's almost like they were written for a PSC Partners conference. The air is sweet and everything is always A-Okay when we're together.

"Come and play
Everything's A-OK
Friendly neighbors there
That's where we meet"

Every year the PSC Partners conference changes locations and, this year, we're in sunny Sacramento, the capital of California. It's a place known for an abundance of sunshine and nothing could be more apropos in this particular case.

Too often PSC can make us feel like we're in the shadows, like we have to search for sunlight and happiness. We're others. We're alone and we're trying to navigate a world in which we're the Oscar the Grouches of Sesame Street, the ones who are always left out of the fun and freedom the rest of the world so easily enjoys.

We're stuck in our little "trashcans" dealing with what our bodies have handed us and have trouble realizing that all we have to do is accept the wonders of the world in order to feel we're more than and not less than.

At a PSC Partners conference, there's just no chance to feel like an outsider. We come from all over the world and speak many different languages. We're in all stages and all have different levels of knowledge about PSC and what it means. Some of us are well-informed, some of us just beginning our PSCer journeys. It doesn't make a difference.

Upon walking in, the love is so overwhelming that there's no chance to feel estranged or removed and the warmth is so empowering that we simply can't shut our lids tight and not experience it all.

Whether we itch or can't get through the day without a nap or a caregiver, there's somebody else who not only gets it but who lives it. There are real-life experiences, answers, empathy and compassion and it's all there just for all of us.

We're not just strangers in the same place because of circumstances; we're family, caregivers, and PSCers.

We're one and the same, brothers and sisters together in a fight for all of our lives and determined to find the joy and power in each and every day.

"It's a magic carpet ride
Every door will open wide
To happy people like you--
Happy people like
What a beautiful sunny day"

Every conference includes experts in the field and this one is no different. We've got doctors from a renowned PSC clinic attending, researchers who are dedicated to helping us unravel the mysteries of PSC, experts in hepatology. We have psychologists who know the best ways in which we can help ourselves understand the enigma of our illness and what PSC is doing to our bodies and minds.

We have physicians and PSCers alike who are all too ready and willing to share the ways in which we can be proactive and ask all the right questions of our medical facilities back home.

We have question and answer panels and a chance to make our voices heard. We discuss the ups and downs of searching for a cure and all the aspects that worry us and bring us cheer when it comes to discoveries that are being made every single day. All of this is vitally important.

But perhaps even more so, we're together, PSCers and caregivers. We laugh and we cry. There may occasionally be tears streaming down our faces but also laughter so loud that it's hard to believe that we're an alcohol free group dealing with the realities of a disease for which there is really no known treatment or a cure as of yet.

We're free to be ourselves in a way that is judgment free and unavailable anywhere else on the planet. Every cell, every breath, every thought is lit up with love and understanding and when there's fear or doubt or worry, there are hundreds of willing shoulders to lean on and arms to wrap around you.

It's okay to be a PSCer. It's okay to be scared. It's okay to be you, no matter what that means.

"Sunny Day
Sweepin' the clouds away
On my way to where the air is sweet
Can you tell me how to get,
How to get to Sesame Street..."

The air is sweet at a PSC Partners conference. And even better, like the famed Sesame Street, we are all neighbors no matter where we come from. We're bonded like Bert and Ernie, feel over 8 feet tall like Big Bird and are free to revel in the little joys and victories like Cookie Monster when he finds a cookie.

For those that have been to a conference before, you know all too well that it changes you down to your very core, making life at once easier to deal with and so much more hopeful.

For those of you who haven't yet experienced it, please join us. I guarantee you won't regret it. You may feel as though all hope is lost, but the sun shines bright here and the clouds really do get swept away.

Oh, and the best part: our version of Sesame Street, is without end. It stretches from Israel to Australia, Louisiana to Victoria, Stockholm to South Dakota and Florida to Fiji. It's without end and we've definitely got room for you on our street and in our lives.

Three Cheers for PSC Partners Conferences!
Sandi Pearlman, The Duct, Winter 2012, pages 9-10

Did you ever watch that old TV show, "Cheers," the one with Sam and Diane, Carla, Cliff and Norm? It's about a bunch of people whose lives revolve around a bar...at least on the surface. Okay. I know, I know, you're already thinking I've flipped my lid writing about a TV show based on a bar in a PSC newsletter of all places, but bear with me for a second.

Because, you see, while Cheers was, in fact, about a group of (perhaps) high-functioning alcoholics and those who waited on them, it was also about a family, people who loved each other and really got each other even when the outside world didn't play fair. It also happens to have a phenomenal theme song* and every single year as the PSC conference rolls closer and closer, it pops into my head. Now, it could be that I've spent too much time with insomnia and Nick-at-Nite (we'll just pretend for the sake of this article that I'm not actually old enough to have seen them when they originally aired), but I think it's more than that.

You see, in the real world, I'm the other. I need a transplant. I have a rare disease. I itch. I'm swollen. I can't sleep and my brain occasionally forgets helpful things like where I am or what I've been doing or the word for "cat." But at the conference, none of that matters. I'm not the other. I'm one and the same in the best of all possible ways. And you know what, you will be, too.

In a world where everyone is constantly judging everyone else, the conference is this lovely oasis in the storm. It's Happy Hour, if you'll pardon the drinking pun. You can scratch, need daytime naps, forget your words and even pass out (although we'd much prefer you conscious) and nobody will judge you. If you happen to be having one of those days where you scratch until you bleed, you won't find judgment or even pity at a PSCP conference. Instead, you're much more likely to find the person next to you offering up a tissue and commiserating about how awful it is to feel like fireants have taken up residence just under your skin. One look at a conference agenda will tell you that PSC is no laughing matter. Our topics range the scope from genetics to MELD, CCA to Urso, Transplant and Depression and back and forth and everywhere in between. But lest you feel as though the conference is just about the tough and cold, hard facts of having an incurable illness, let me let you in on another little secret. PSC Partners conferences are also notorious for their laughter and fun.

My little sister--now not so little at 34, I realize--refers to the conferences as the best time she has all year. Another PSCer I know calls them her family reunions--with family she actually wants to see. And yet another PSCer has actually told his transplant team that they'd better make sure he's either transplanted before or after the conference because he's absolutely not missing one. The reason PSCP conferences inspire such loyalty and reverence is simple. Everyone is welcome, wanted and accepted. There's no need to pretend to be a 'healthy' person and try to take a bite of something when you're too nauseous to eat or to try and pretend anything else for that matter. You're in a room where everyone is gathered together for the same thing, to become better informed about this disease that has brought us all to this place in time and to find a way to defeat it. We're not powerless. We're powerful. We don't need liquid courage or fortifying. We're enough. No matter how weak we sometimes feel in regular life, here, together, we're strong.

This year, I'm the co-chair for the conference. I can tell you firsthand that the speakers we have lined up are truly phenomenal and to say that they're widely regarded as some of, if not the, best in their fields is not an overstatement. But you know what matters just as much to me, they care. Not one of the 'demigods' of PSC has had even the tiniest bit of an ego. In fact, just the opposite. They've been gracious and questioning and really want to work with PSC Partners to give all of us the answers we need and to address the subjects that we most care about. For many PSCers, names like Lindor and Gores, Lazaridis, Kane and Talwalkar are just those words behind authors' bylines of numerous medical articles. For me, and I know for all of you attending, they're about to become so much more. They'll no longer be nameless, faceless doctors working out in space somewhere. No, they'll be the ones seated next to you, holding your hand, Cliff to your Norm or Sam to your Diane. They'll be your Cheers-ing section and you'll certainly be glad you came.

Making your way in the world today takes everything you've got.
Taking a break from all your worries, sure would help a lot.
Wouldn't you like to get away?
Sometimes you want to go
Where everybody knows your name,
and they're always glad you came.
You wanna be where you can see,
our troubles are all the same
You wanna be where everybody knows
Your name.

The Love Letter

Sandi Pearlman, The Duct, Summer 2012-I, pages 10-11

Here's the thing, I don't know anybody who doesn't truly, secretly, proudly and completely adore love letters. I mean, what's not to love? A love letter is emotion in its truest form. It's thought combined with action and the care it takes to put pen to paper or fingers to keyboard. It's somebody taking a minute (or 10 or 20) of their time to profess their innermost appreciation for another. There isn't a person alive who can resist the allure of love no matter how hard they may try. And for me, for many, PSC Partners conferences are a love letter of sorts. It's all of us, taking time from our overly busy and hectic lives and putting down obstacles and illnesses and demands to be with each other come what may. For we know, this all-too-short weekend is our chance to profess our love and dedication to one another and our commitment to curing not just ourselves, but all of us. We're together in the fight, whatever it takes, not because it's the PSC Partners slogan; but because it describes what's written in our hearts and souls, in our very cells. It is the essence of a love letter, eternal, beautiful, powerful.

I've been accused of overstating the amount of love in our group. I've been told that what I'm saying simply can't be true. But you know what I hear most on the subject from first-time attendees and those doubters, I hear that I was right. I hear their joy as they tell me they now know I wasn't overstating, selling them flowery promises with wilted stems at the core. There's simply no such thing as isolation at the conference. From the hugs and greetings as one enters the door to the handholding and tissue sharing in breakout groups or as we listen to sometimes dire statistics, the love is there. It bubbles out in song--lots of songs this year--and in stories and in shared moments. It's there in the knowledge that our loads are much lighter because we have everyone's shoulders to share the weight and it's no longer our battle alone.

As anyone who has ever been in love can attest, love doesn't just come straight at you charging like a bull in a china shop. It caresses, like words on a page, until you're so enveloped you can barely remember what life was like before. And once you're open to the love and beauty in the world, it pours forth, even from unexpected sources. At this year's conference alone, there were doctors who were mobbed like rock stars as they patiently answered questions and listened to stories. We loved them and their time, expertise and attention and they proved again and again that they're more than physicians. They showed us in words and in actions that they're comrades in the fight, aiming to cure PSC and stop its ravaging effects before it's too late. Then there are our sponsors, some who attended and others who couldn't, who give of themselves to support us both in spirit and in funding to allow us to keep our conferences accessible to so many. And there are all of us, PSCers and caregivers from all corners of the world. We come together to make ourselves more informed, more connected and to share of ourselves and our experiences with those who understand us most, those who are just like us; those who know the initials PSC like we know the back of our hands and who know that we're more than a diagnosis, even when our bodies try to prove the very opposite.

This was my fifth conference and, for me, the love just gets stronger and stronger. It defies language barriers and sometimes grim information. It doesn't matter if we've known each other for five years or five minutes. As Renée Zellweger famously said, "You had me at hello." PSCers, caregivers, you all had me at hello. You make me feel inspired and brave. You remind me that I not only can survive PSC, but I can thrive with PSC; that we all can.

The thing about love letters is that they stay forever etched upon our hearts and minds long past the moments we first encounter them. The words and feelings imprint themselves in our memories and in our cells becoming a part of us that we can call upon when things get rough. Our conferences may only be one all-too-short weekend a year, but as anyone who has ever attended knows, they are a love letter that keeps on giving, bringing us back to special moments and the love shared time and again. They're love letters that we keep tucked away in our hearts until we meet again, written in the most beautiful script and forever meaningful. Sending love until we meet again in Pittsburgh. Forever yours, *Sandi.*

To Conference or Not to Conference?

Sandi Pearlman, The Duct, Summer 2013, pages 8-9

I wasn't going to go. If you know me, you know that's no small thing. I half expect when the vampires take my blood one of these days that I'll get a call saying, "Um, you know, we're wondering something. You see, our techs are finding all these little *PSC Partners* floating in your bloodstream like some kind of madcap chicken soup...." So, when I say I wasn't going to go, even if you don't know me, maybe you can appreciate the gravity of those words and feelings.

Why? Well, I wasn't sure I had it in me, physically, emotionally or otherwise. I was just plain, old spent. I'd need to negotiate endless doctors arguments against leaving Clinic grounds/territory--I'm listed and rather ill--and I'd have to negotiate the terms of leaving and then I'd probably end up in the hospital upon return. Plus, how was I going to enjoy myself, run my sessions, do all I needed to do when I'm so far past empty that the red line gave up on the gauge and called out for pizza instead? But, pal, boy am I glad I went and here's why: You all rock. We rock. PSCers are amazingly extraordinary people and stunningly wonderful in so many ways.

Whether eating pizza, going up to The Incline or just hanging around in the lobby, our group is restorative, loving, loud (really loud) and so connected even strangers know upon seeing us that we're family. We share stories and secrets. Fears come out to see the light of day and we learn they're not quite so scary after all. We hold the hands of people whom two days ago we didn't even know but are now forever a part of our lives, inexplicably intertwined through this madness called PSC which only those touched by it can truly understand. We say we're PSCers and caregivers, but we're all caregivers. Not once did I look around at the conference and see somebody alone. Not once was somebody looking for a warm embrace unable to find it. And the camaraderie is evident, we miss each other, need each other, crave this world that restores us all in our sameness and our abilities to lose our inhibitions and just be. We scratch; we cry; we laugh; we vomit; we dance; we go through box after box of Kleenex and we love. Most of all, we love.

At the conference, it doesn't matter if you're 13 or 33, 40 or 75, we're all the same, even in our differences because we choose, on a level not even our subconscious recognizes as decision making, to recognize each other. During sessions, we devour information and look to the experts to fill gaps in our knowledge or teach us something new. Out of the sessions, we sing (boy, do we ever) and we shop and we savor each moment because we know how fleeing they are. Those of us who normally sleep 18 hours a day or can't get up off the couch are suddenly going out to get sandwiches at 2:00 a.m. because we can't bear the thought of missing a moment. We literally exhaust ourselves for that one more second to spend together.

And goodbye is never easy. We know it's not forever, that another conference will come around, but still it hurts. Tears flow and hearts break a little knowing that the next morning we won't wake up and see those we've come to love and rely upon. But we know, too, that the invisible tether will hold strong. That we'll connect via technology (shameless plug for PSC Partners Facebook), via telephone calls and visits and, of course, the next conference.

So, I thank you. Thank all of you. Because, you see, you've restored me. You've given me strength to take with me and memories to keep me laughing (anyone who missed Karaoke, please, don't make that mistake again!). When I go into my next appointment, I'm not walking in alone. You're there with me, holding my hand and whispering words of encouragement. And when the news isn't good and I want to cry, your shoulders are ready for me to lean on. We're never in this thing all alone because we have each other. My cells may say PSC Partners, but they also bear each of your names and I hold them close. They shelter me, comfort me, and remind me that no matter what the war against PSC brings, that we're all together in this fight, whatever it takes. We're stronger than PSC. We're stronger than anything thrown at us and together we'll find a cure. You'll save me and I'll save you because, quite simply, that's what family does.

IT'S ALL ABOUT THE NAP
Sandi Pearlman, The Duct, Fall 2008, page 29

It's hard enough to be in your 20s and 30s. Everyone tells you that they're the greatest times of your life: you leave home for the first time, you find a job, contemplate starting a family with that special someone, etc. It's a lot for anyone to deal with. And then you add PSC. Wet blanket, anyone?

Just at a time where we're supposed to be exploring ourselves, going out, meeting people, we PSCers face an energy crisis.

In our 20s, we're experiencing college, leaving home and living on our own for the first time. It's a time to go wild, to be free to try a million different things on the path to finding out who we are. You're supposed to fall in love with all the wrong people, shut down bars and parties, hang out at diners until the wee hours of the morning.

Only problem is, you can't seem to stay up past 8:00, you're so tired that holding a conversation is tantamount to climbing Mt. Everest and the only bedroom activity you're interested in involves you, your comforter, and some nice long Zzzzs.

As to those trips to the local bar, well, you're pretty sure eventually somebody's going to notice that the only drink that ever touches your hand is an orange soda or a rum and coke minus the rum. And pick-up lines: "Hi, I'm Jack, I can't drink, I feel the need to sleep for hours on end, I itch in the oddest places and, oh, yeah, I have an incurable disease that will most likely lead to transplant. How about I buy you a coke?"

In our 30s, we're supposed to be settling down, solidifying our careers, making lifelong commitments and starting families. Our peers are happy to trot along to the local bar for a quick pint and not make it home 'til five past midnight while we're struggling to stay awake for the 7:00 news or fighting our urge to just let the kids forage in the pantry for whatever they may find and call it dinner surprise. And that's just for those of us who even have the energy to work, leave the house or have kids.

A quick drink with the boss seems like the road to promotion, but how to explain why that's just not quite possible without giving your boss details best left private or being labeled a recovering alcoholic or prude.

And let us not forget the romantic side of things. First, we have to have the energy to go out and meet someone, not to mention hold a sparkling conversation if and when we do.

Then, that partner has to remain unfazed by the whole transplant thing and, on top of that, be more than a little understanding when we're just too tired to be in the mood. If you know someone who fits this description and has decent health insurance, by all means, send him my way and check to see how many siblings he has for the rest of us out there.

Here's the thing, it's cute to have nap time when you're in kindergarten. It's fine for execs to power nap in the afternoon. It's not so fine when you're so exhausted all the time that your version of a nap lasts three or four hours and you're still exhausted upon waking.

So, what's a PSCer to do? Do we proudly wear Ts that shout slogans like "I [heart] Naps" or warn our dates, spouses, and friends that if we fall asleep on them it really isn't the company? Should we all hang out with narcoleptics so they just won't notice?

I guess there are no easy answers, at least none that I can come up with at the moment and it is getting close to nap time . . .

The Glass Half Full

Sandi Pearlman, The Duct, Spring 2009, pages 25-26

As I'm sitting here writing this, I am mere hours away from my 33rd birthday. I suppose I could be out whooping it up, drowning the last of 32 in glasses of wine and beer held aloft by well-wishing friends and family.

Instead, I sit at home on my couch and find myself reflecting. To look at me, I look like an average girl, perhaps a little too thin, maybe in need of a haircut, but rather unremarkable all the same. No one would ever look at me and think, well, that girl there is fighting an incurable disease.

And yet, that's exactly what I am doing, what we are really doing (minus the girl for some of us!). We're fighters. We're given an impossible task: beat an incurable disease and live life without letting it destroy us, and, still, we march on.

I had a pre-interview with one of the counselors on my transplant team. For those of you who haven't yet had the pleasure, they ask you a lot of questions, try to gauge how emotionally ready you'll be when and if the big day comes, freak you out about finances and planning and that kind of a thing.

In any case, my counselor (who would have a conniption if she read this and found I called her "counselor" rather than case worker or social worker) asked me what was the best thing that ever happened to me.

I responded that it probably hadn't happened yet. She frowned and asked me, well, what's the worst thing that ever happened to you. I said, well, it probably hasn't happened yet. Her response, I swear, was that she thinks I need therapy.

See, she couldn't understand why I wouldn't say PSC was the worst thing that ever happened to me. She couldn't grasp why it wasn't waiting there on the tip of my tongue like a cat after cheese and eager to drop from my lips. But the truth is, I find my answer hopeful that there's more to come, that PSC isn't the defining characteristic of my life.

Don't get me wrong, PSC sucks. I'm going to go out on a limb here and say that there isn't a single one of us who would choose to have the disease or keep the disease in the face of another positive option. But the fact is, in some ways PSC is both one of the best and one of the worst things in my life.

Before you all scream that the therapy idea was right, let me explain. The itching, nausea, RUQ pain, shortened life expectancy, etc., is more than a drag. It absolutely has to be worse than Chinese water torture.

But PSC also gives us an edge. We're not like the dude on the couch in the lounge somewhere thinking he has an unlimited lifetime to make choices and say sorry and make love and dream dreams. We know life is precious. It's ours for this day and hopefully for the next and, damn, if we're going to waste it.

We might be too tired to hit a party, can't go out for a beer with the pals or itch in inappropriate places at inconvenient times, but we know the value of the times we can go out, the friends we have and the blessed itch-free nanoseconds we're occasionally awarded.

I'm a glass half full kind of girl. In fact, some of my friends say relentlessly so. They insist if life threw at them what it's thrown at me, at us, that they'd curl up and die or spend all day crying in a corner and asking why me.

Well, the truth is, there are days when I want to curl up in a corner and whine why me and bawl my eyes out until I've lost at least four pounds of water weight. But what's the use?

At the end of the day, unless you've got a better connection to God than I do, you're probably not going to get an answer. So, as 33 rapidly approaches, instead of wallowing in the have-nots of being sick and lacking energy and facing what could be years of poking and prodding and ERCPs and colonoscopies and the like, I find myself smiling.

I still may need therapy, but PSC has taught me to appreciate what is good. I know who my true friends are, I feel the warmth and the love as they and my family rally around me. I laugh as they jokingly refer to PSC as Pearlman, Sandi Cure. I think, all in all, I'm a lucky girl.

I may have a disease that requires a fight every single day of my life, I may be on a first name basis with more doctors than I can shake a stick at and have my own shelf in the pharmacy, but it also allows me to see all the things worth fighting for that might otherwise have gone unnoticed.

Thirty-three brings with it the first sign of wrinkles, a few gray hairs and a peace of mind that I can make a difference in my own life. I can raise money to fight PSC, to look for a cure. I can curl up and nap on a picnic blanket while my friends play Monopoly and drink wine.

I can be me without worrying what the world will think because I know every moment is precious and there's no guarantee that tomorrow will be there...and if it is and I'm itching and exhausted, well, I know I've survived it before and I'll most likely survive it again today.

***

Now on a completely unrelated matter, a plea to all of you 20 and 30 somethings reading this column. I know most of you've heard us go on and on about the upcoming conference in Chicago on May 1-3, 2009, and, perhaps, about last year's conference in Jacksonville.

There's a reason for that. Quite simply, we want you to come! I'd say for a large number of us PSCers, especially when first diagnosed, we feel all alone out there in the world when it comes to all things PSC-related.

We hang on tight to our internet PSC Partners friends and rely on them for understanding, shared experiences, compassion, a good kick in the pants when needed; but, perhaps, we've never really met another PSCer face to face.

Well, the conference is your chance. It might seem scary, intimidating, depressing or just a waste of time; but I promise you, it's not.

Last year was my first conference. I went to it on the urging of my doctor . . . and was glad I did. I not only made fabulous friends, one of whom I talk to so often we almost need walkie-talkies, but just the experience of sitting down and talking to somebody who really, truly understands what it's like to have PSC is life-altering.

Suddenly, you're not the freak who can't stop scratching or can't make it through the day without a nap, you're one of many who can't stop scratching and can't get through the day without a nap. There's plenty of food, conversation and fun to go along with all the medical advice, research updates and statistics...and if that doesn't convince you...well, there's always the free pens and pill holders and such from our sponsors.

Just think, peace of mind, new friends and free gifts, I ask you, how can you beat that?

Meme x 2
Sandi and Karen Pearlman, The Duct, Fall 2010, pages 25-32

There's this thing that happens every September. It's not a big event in the grand scheme of things. It's not going to fall on many calendars with bright, red circles around it and, chances are, you've never even heard of its existence. It's called Invisible Illness Week., or more technically, National Invisible Chronic Illness Awareness Week, but that's a mouthful, so let's go with the shorthand version, shall we?

IIW (nice, right, I even shortened the shorthand!) was started in 2002 by a woman named Lisa Copen and I'm sure there are lots of other interesting factoids, but they're not pertinent and I'm a PSCer and realize that life and time are precious, as are our attention spans, so let's not dwell on any of the mysteries of its origin right now.

What is relevant is that every year IIW asks people with chronic illnesses to do a "meme," which is essentially their interpretation of a memo all about me (or you as the case may be). In these 30 questions, they ask those with chronic illnesses to open up and bare their souls and share with the world what it's like to be invisible and ailing.

I've done it and it's cathartic and nerve-wracking and freeing and depressing and about 100 other adjectives. But something's always bothered me: Why is it only for those diagnosed with a chronic illness? Who knows better than a PSCer that while the disease may lie in our particular bodies, it's a community diagnosis? PSC affects our friends and families and spouses and siblings and it just doesn't seem fair that there's no meme for them.

So, this year, I'm changing that and I'm challenging you to change it, too. Below, you'll find my answers to the wordy 30 and those of my little sis's (with the questions modified a bit for non-PSCers or PSCEers* as my sis and I call 'em). Once you're done reading (the WHOLE newsletter, of course), head over to [PSC Partners Facebook] (there's a Discussion Board heading all ready and waiting for you!) to find the questions and fill out your 30 and urge your friends or family members to do the same.

Then, share them on PSC Partners FB or on your own Facebook pages. Send them out to your e-mail list. Revel in the fact that you're accomplishing the impossible: you're making the invisible visible and you don't need a certain day, month, or time to make that more than okay. Talk about Power, Strength and Courage.

From Sandi: 30 Things About My Invisible Illness You May Not Know: Some Time in The Life of a PSCer

1. The illness I live with is: Primary Sclerosing Cholangitis (PSC) as well as Ulcerative Colitis, Gastroparesis and more.

2. I was diagnosed with it in the year: Honestly, I don't even know anymore. I was so sick the whole thing is a blur. I'm guessing it was 2006 or 2007.

3. But I had symptoms since: I'd been sick off and on for years and one doctor after another told me it was just "stress." I eventually became so ill that I lost the ability to walk, went into renal failure and was, quite literally according to the docs, three days from dead before I got an actual diagnosis. Guess I proved them wrong about that three days from dead thing though, huh? :)

4. The biggest adjustment I've had to make is: Every single day with PSC is a million little battles fought in a (currently) unwinable war. I miss my privacy and independence. I miss my savings (being ill costs an awful lot). I miss my energy. I miss my cellphone being filled up with friends' names instead of doctors' names and nurse coordinators and transplant secretaries and pharmacies and the like. I miss being able to count on my body and my brain to work the ways they always had in the past. Depending on the day or the moment, any or all of these things are my biggest adjustment.

5. Most people assume: I'm healthy (unless they know me). Even those who know I'm ill generally think things are far better or more stable than they truly are. I think that's one part because they're not capable of understanding (thank goodness, because it means they've never experienced something like PSC themselves) and one part my being unwilling to always show the world exactly how tough things can be.

6. The hardest part about mornings are: Um, waking up? How are we defining "morning?" :) Again, depends on the day for me. Sometimes, it's getting up to feed the cat and finding that by the time I've walked to the kitchen my energy for the day is already gone. Sometimes it's the fact that I'm okay with "morning" being whenever I decide to wake up, even if it's 5:00 p.m., and others in my household are not. (Which I still can't quite figure out. Why do they wake me? If it's to check and see if I'm breathing, I clearly am or I wouldn't be sleeping and if I wasn't, they couldn't wake me anyhow, and if I'm sleeping, clearly I need sleep more than anything else! Don't they watch CSI? Don't they know if I was dead my eyes would be opened, not closed?)

[7.] My favorite medical TV show is: General Hospital, although these days that's more of a Mobster show, so I'll go with Grey's Anatomy in that case :)

8. A gadget I couldn't live without is: my laptop. I love you, my beautiful Mac! :)

9. The hardest part about nights are: Insomnia. I'm beyond exhausted so much of the time and I'm completely befuddled by the fact that my body won't let me sleep. I'm too exhausted to watch tv or talk or anything other than to stare into space and still sometimes sleep won't come! What's up with that? I don't need Mr. Sandman to bring me a dream, just a little restorative shuteye would be nice every once in a while.

10. Each day I take 20+ pills & vitamins. And that's on a good day. If it's a rough day or I'm having a cholangitis attack, that number shoots up closer to the 30+ mark and some of those pills I take more than once a day.

11. Regarding alternative treatments: I have tried so many of them. I'd say the one that works the best for me is mindfulness, trying to stay present and enjoying what life has to offer whether that's a great TV show, a conversation with a friend or even just laughing at my rascal of a cat. Part of mindfulness is also forgiving myself for things I didn't choose. So, I'm upset when my body won't let me do what I want, but I work on not dwelling there and instead I search for the good points to whatever the case may be. Oh, and chocolate sometimes helps a lot. :)

12. If I had to choose between an invisible illness or visible I would choose: They both have their drawbacks, right? Nobody wants to look horrible, but I will say that the days when I'm in my wheelchair or exceptionally pale or thin, people do seem to be kinder, more willing to cut me some slack and accept that I'm sick rather than when I'm walking around and feeling horrid but they can't tell. The "healthy looking days" people tell me I must be feeling well or they think I'm exaggerating how bad things are or even faking the whole thing. It puts me in the position of feeling defensive, which I hate, so I try hard to remember that most people don't mean anything other than kindness and support. Hopefully that counts as an answer! :)

13. Regarding working and career: I was devastated to lose my job when I became ill. Being in your 30s and unable to work is humiliating, difficult and hard to explain to people whose first question is generally, "What do you do?" I know my body isn't capable of what it once was and that regular "work" is not an option for me. But I still miss it (or aspects of it) almost every day! But as my friends and family tell me, I do still work. I might not get a paycheck, but the dividends are far greater. Fighting to eradicate PSC and being a part of PSC Partners fulfills my heart and soul in ways I consider myself truly blessed to experience!

14. People would be surprised to know: I'm pretty much an open book. Hmm, should I worry that I have no mystery left? Um....

15. The hardest thing to accept about my new reality has been: that there's no normality. When most people wake up in the morning, they can expect their day to go a certain way to a certain degree. They expect to have the energy to get out of bed. They expect to be able to keep down their breakfast and remember the word for "car" or "phone." They expect that if they've made plans, even little ones like throwing the wash in the dryer, that they'll be able to accomplish those goals. For a PSCer, we can't count on any of those things. Despite our wants, our bodies sometimes just say no to things we need and want to do. In terms of doing the wash though, my best advice is to screw the laundry and just buy a lot of underwear. I'm a fan of Victoria's Secret myself, but your underwear is your choice. :)

16. Something I never thought I could do with my illness that I did was: Turn it into a positive. Don't get me wrong, there's PLENTY of suckage with PSC (hmm, I all of a sudden went Pauly Shore mid-90s on that one, huh?). Anyhow, PSC isn't fun and it isn't something I'd wish on even my worst enemy, well . . . :) PSC brings so many negatives it practically requires its own ZIP code, but it can also bring good. In my case, it brought closer, real friendships and focus on the people, issues and things that really matter to me. It brought a realization that my life is mine to choose and I can wallow or laugh or sleep or play or see each day as a new possibility instead

of one day closer to not having any more days, which, if you think about it, is a boat we're all in anyhow, might as well enjoy the ride and not drive yourself crazy scrambling for a paddle.

[17.] The commercials about my illness: are nonexistent. Hopefully, one day that will change.

18. Something I really miss doing since I was diagnosed is: Hmm, I miss being ridiculously reliable. I miss knowing that if I say I'll be somewhere that I know my body will let me be there and my brain will be on board. As to what do I miss doing, I miss just sitting down to write and not having to really think and knowing my words would be there for me without my even acknowledging them. Oh, and I miss white water rafting, too. :)

19. It was really hard to have to give up: this idea that I am/was what I do. I had to learn to separate myself from a traditional job-titled society where you're measured by your paygrade and office size or the alphabet soup of letters behind your name. I'm actually still working on this one and I lost my ability to work and my job around 4 years ago now. (By the way, I don't mean to imply anything bad about people who are their work. Let's face it, whatever part of me isn't water and liver disease is entirely PSC Partners, it's just that I had to learn to separate and realize I can be more than just whatever my job title may be. And if you think that's easy or an odd thing to miss, try introducing yourself to somebody new and don't talk at all about what you do for a full 5 minutes. Bet it'll feel like 40!)

20. A new hobby I have taken up since my diagnosis is: Facebook. Oh, Heaven bless Facebook! :)

[21] If I could have one day of feeling normal again I would: Is it sad that I don't even know? I think the word "normal" should be in quotes in the question above. Who defines normal anyhow?

22. My illness has taught me: Appreciation for what life has to offer. It's taught me to love with a bigger heart and listen on a grander scale. It's taught me that sometimes some of the most wonderful things in the world are born out of some of the most devastating.

23. Want to know a secret? One thing people say that gets under my skin is: Do I have to pick just one? I hate people telling me if I had accepted religion or religious figures properly I wouldn't be sick. I can't stand when somebody tells me they know a "surefire" cure (like rubbing sesame oil on my feet is really going to fix my PSC. Grr)! I'm annoyed when people offer advice and I thank them and then they still keep pressuring me every single time they see me. Okay, I'm really hung up on the sesame oil lady, but she drives me crazy! I'm horrified when people tell me I must have invited illness in. Why would anyone say such a thing? Oh, I also don't like it when people say the words "moist" or "ooze," but that's just because they sound nasty. :)

24. But I love it when people: remember I'm a person and not just a "sick chick." I love when people laugh with me and show me they care and ask questions because they want answers and

not because they're trying to be polite. I love it when people surprise me with their generosity and understanding and I love it when people remember I'm not an only child and that my sister still exists and matters and that my parents are more than just the parents of a chronically ill daughter. I love it when people see me as a person first rather than a sick person and then, if at all, a person.

25. My favorite motto, scripture, quote that gets me through tough times is: Laugh, don't cry. Is that really narcissistic, to quote myself? It's what I live by though!

26. When someone is diagnosed I'd like to tell them: that they're not alone, they have a hand to hold and a shoulder to cry on and a partner in the millions of battles and wars PSC puts us through on a daily basis.

27. Something that has surprised me about living with an illness is: The irregularity of it all and the expense of it all. Also, the guilt can be a lot to take. All of the sudden, I went from independent to a burden (or potential burden, anyway). It's tough to reconcile all of that guilt.

28. The nicest thing someone did for me when I wasn't feeling well was: There have been so many things, my little sister staying with me in my hospital bed when I couldn't walk or move and literally, physically and emotionally, getting me through the day, my parents spending hours and days in ugly, uncomfortable hospital chairs eating nasty vending machine food, my friends who constantly check in and never make me feel bad when I'm too ill to do something we've planned. There are a million and one reasons to be grateful every single day for all the love headed my way from family and friends, even if sometimes I'm too ill, exhausted or scared to remember that.

29. I'm involved with Invisible Illness Week because: everybody needs to know they're not invisible and that they matter. Because it's horrible to walk into a doctor's office and have them stare at you blankly and say they've never heard of your disease or give you unforgivably wrong information. Because it's our chance as PSCers to tell the real truth about what our lives are like and show others they're not alone and still others that we may be down occasionally, but we're definitely not out!

[30.] The fact that you read this list makes me feel: honored, grateful, and nervous! There's a lot of personal stuff here! :)

From Karen: 30 Things About My Invisible Illness You May Not Know: Some Time in The Life of A PSCer

The illness I live with is: PSC

My sister was diagnosed with it in the year: How long has it been now?

Upon hearing the diagnosis I felt: Scared, confused, but mostly ready to find out what PSC was and what could be done to fight it.

The biggest adjustment I've had to make is: Allowing for more understanding regarding how tired, sick, full of pain, etc., my sister is. I went from the bratty little sister to trying to be more of a support system.

Most people assume: That I grieve daily and I may. However, I do not think about PSC all day every day. In so many ways this disease has allowed a closer bond to form between my sister and me. It has allowed me to see her for the strong and inspiring person that she truly is.

Here's what I usually tell people: PSC is an autoimmune disease that affects the liver and bile ducts and, if you really want to know all the details, go to www.pscpartners.org. Or if somebody asks me the "How is Sandi doing?" question, I usually respond that she is still alive. After being so close to death early on and fighting her way back, I consider the fact that she's still alive a pretty miraculous thing. Maybe it's not the best answer; but it does get frustrating to be asked that question so often, especially since there are good-ish days and bad days, but no real "relief" days.

My favorite medical TV show is: I guess Grey's only b/c Sandi watches it and, therefore, I end up watching it. Otherwise, it probably would've been House. I love me a sarcastic man :)

A gadget I couldn't live without is: my camera. It allows me the outlet I need in life.

The hardest part about living with PSC is: Watching the toll it takes on my family. While there are positives I can see, it is hard to see the years it has added to my parents and the pain and suffering that my sister deals with on a daily basis.

I hope my PSCer knows: How inspired I am by her, all that she deals with and with such a positive attitude and, also, how she has become such a driving force among other PSCers to keep their spirits up and give them a place to vent and let them know they are not alone.

Regarding alternative treatments: I think, why not, what do you have to lose? Of course, it's not my body in this particular case. :)

One thing that surprised me about life with a PSCer is: How much more valuable a laughing fit can be or simply time spent together, although not necessarily the Victoria's Secret runs :)

PSC makes me feel: Angry, upset, bitter.

However, PSCers make me feel inspired and amazed.

People would be surprised to know: That while I would never wish PSC on anyone, I can see quite a bit of beauty that this diagnosis has brought into our lives.

I'm embarrassed to admit: That at times I forget how sick my sister is and get annoyed by the fact that she cannot accomplish simple things.

I feel most reassured when: I see that Sandi has been active on Facebook, then I know she's having a good day. :)

The commercials about my illness: What commercials? This is a problem. We need to get the word out there!

Something I really miss doing with my PSCer: Simple things like apple picking, walking around the neighborhood, going to events, seeing her in action in the library, etc. While we can still do these things, it is with much more difficulty for Sandi.

It was really hard to have to give up: That feeling that my sister was always going to be around, that sense of security.

To deal with the bad days I: Usually go to the gym, hike, or kayak, to rid myself of any sadness and/or stress.

If my PSCer could have one day of feeling normal again I'd want them to: Relax, do anything she wants, even if it was just sitting around watching television enjoying a pain free day. However, I seriously doubt, that sitting around would be her choice activity if that wonderful "normal" day were to come.

This illness has taught me: To appreciate everyone, namely my sister/family and just how strong people can be.

Want to know a secret? One thing people say that gets under my skin is: "How is Sandi doing?" I know this sounds terrible, but I get asked that question 20 times a day by the general public. While I love that so many people care, how lovely would it be if they followed that question up with, "What can I do to help?"

But I love it when people: Take the time to learn what PSC is, ask questions and care enough to get involved.

My favorite motto, scripture, quote that gets me through tough times is: Hmmm, not sure I have one. As a general rule, I am not a worrier and that gets me through everything. Why should I worry and cause myself all that stress?

When someone is diagnosed I'd like to tell them: You are not alone. And then I'd direct them to the FB site as well as strongly encourage them to come to the next conference. I look forward to the conference every year. Every PSCer and caregiver should have the experience of being in a room with so many others in a similar situation.

Something that has surprised me about living with an illness is: The positives that come with it. Granted, I'm not the one with the actual disease; but, as mentioned earlier, PSC has made me appreciate my sister and own healthy life even more and it's definitely brought my family even closer.

I know I'm appreciated when: I can make my family laugh. Laughter is one thing that this disease tries to diminish, but as Sandi always says, "You can laugh or cry. So, choose laugh."

I'm involved with Invisible Illness Week because: I love my sister and the many other PSCers I have met.

The fact that you read this list makes me feel: It doesn't make me feel any certain way, but hopefully it makes other caregivers feel less alone.

***

For those that are interested, these lists were made without any input from the other and only combined together once we'd each individually completed them...oh, and I think I've officially been outed for my obsession with Victoria's Secret. :)

*PSCEer: the loved one of a PSCer. The E in PSCEer stands for either empathy or envy depending on the situation.

Be a Hero or Heroine and Save the Day:
PSC's First Ever Fundraising Weekend, October 2-4
The Duct, Summer 2009, pages 18-21

Have you ever wanted to be a superhero, you know, rush in and save the day? Be the be all end all to countless men, women and children, swooping in and saving the lives of damsels (and dudemars) in distress?

Well, now you're in luck because being a true superhero is even easier than ever these days and anyone can do it no matter how old, young, tired, itchy and/or sleep-deprived!

So, grab your cape, boots and decoder ring and join us the first weekend in October for our first ever annual PSC Partners "Save the Day!"

We all know that as things stand we're fighting an unstoppable villain. PSC storms in, takes over and there's little we can do to stop it. But every uber-villain thinks they're unstoppable and every superhero knows that the stopping is just a matter of time.

So, PSC might have the upper hand at the moment, but with our team of heroes in the making, it frankly doesn't stand a chance. And when we band together, watch out world! October 2-4 kicks off our first ever Save the Day-athon. So hold those fundraisers. Hit up those friends. Tell those villainous PSC genes they're going down!

On that weekend, the good guys are taking over. So, whether you're gathering up the funds from a year-long fundraiser or holding one for the first time this October, let's make this year's Save the Day one for the history books. Sound good? Great! Super!

Now that you're ready to leap enormous obstacles in a single bound without breaking a sweat, here are a few tips on how to achieve superhero status. I mean, really, there are a million ways. Here's just a few:

For Superheroes who don't want to plan:

It's Jar-ring how much money can accumulate in a spare change jar, swear jar, desk fountain, etc. So, make it a house rule. Even better, see if you can get your pals to make it a house rule, too. Then make it a habit. Every day empty out your pockets, purses and backpacks and toss all the change into your dedicated jar. After a few months or a year, count it all up and donate it to PSC Partners on October 2-4 for research, education, and to get on the path to the cure.

Overachiever Effort: Make a guess. Everyone in the family guesses how much money your jar's going to accumulate by your designated donate date. Whoever comes in closest, does nothing. All other guessers add another $1, $5, whatever you decide, to the donation jar.

Got a job? Do chores? Get an allowance? Well, then you're in luck. You've got everything you need to start earning those super stripes. Donate a portion (or all) of your babysitting/allowance/lawn-mowing/pet-walking money, etc., for a month, two months, a year. Just think, if you donate just $5 a week for an entire year that's $260 towards the cause. Whoa, baby, that's some good progress!

Overachiever Effort: Get friends in on the action. Have all your buddies grab a rake or a lawn-mower and try to outmatch each other. Form your own Babysitter's Club and see how much you can earn as a group. Do extra chores and see how quickly you can reach a set goal!

Take the opportunity. Friends and family not know what to get you for the big day? How about a donation in the amount of your age (or the one you wish you were) to your favorite nonprofit, PSC Partners. Use your Facebook status for good. Announce an upcoming special occasion and ask for donations in lieu of gifts. (Make sure you tell people exactly how to donate!)

Overachiever Effort: Get your friends, family and coworkers to join the generosity. Ask them to use their special days to earn PSC Partners funds as well. Challenge those around you. Write a check for $10 and see how many people you can get to match it with checks of their own.

For Superheroes who are down with the planning:

Well, we all know that when the townsfolk band together amazing things can happen. So, why not start your own spectacular force of friends and neighbors? Use cover charges to your advantage. Hold a karaoke party, a theme party, a movie night. The options are endless. You get a great time with your pals and provide the location/movie/karaoke machine. They get to give to a worthy cause and have a grand time. You can even make it a contest. Charge everyone $5 or $10 to get in and then pick a "winner" for your movie quiz, karaoke contest, costume contest, etc., and provide them with a small prize.

Overachiever Effort: Make it a monthly do.

Get the community involved. Contact your church, temple, school, local businesses, daycares, etc. See if they'd be up for a fundraiser. Ask about a Dress Down Day. Employees pay a set amount and can dress down. They love you, you love them and talk about an awareness booster! You can hold a bake sale, a book sale, a garage sale, a car wash. Hold a battle of the bands, a game night. Go bowling. You can go nuts with DDR or a video game tournament. Hold a Tupperware/Mary Kay/Avon party. The options are endless.

Overachiever Effort: Advertise your fundraiser. Now's not the time to be a shrinking violet. Shout your fundraiser from the rooftops. Call the radio, the local PTAs. If you get one school to agree, try another. See if you can get all the branches of your local library system, every church in the town, etc. The more you ask, the better a chance for a yes!

<u>Eat it up and Dish it out</u>. Hold a dinner party with a silent auction on the side. Ask your friends to bring no-longer needed items and auction them off to each other. It's a total win/win. Everyone gets to donate, get rid of things they don't want and gets a brand new item to take home!

Like pancakes? Spaghetti? Great, hold a breakfast or a dinner. Maybe you can even get a local restaurant to donate the food if you're lucky. A couple bucks "cover charge" and you've got the makings of a mighty tasty fundraiser.

Overachiever Effort: Make a cookbook and sell it at your breakfast/dinner. Ask your friends to bring a friend to your next dinner party. The more people, the more items to auction off and funds and awareness to raise.

For Superheroes who want to end up on cereal boxes:

Take to the skies and shout from the rooftops while you're leaping those buildings in a single bound. Go to several local stores and ask them to donate 10 percent of their profits on Save the Day day. Contact local newspapers and TV stations and ask them to tell your story and mention how people can help while you spread awareness.

Use your church or temple bulletins or your local community newsletter and get the word out on PSC awareness and let them know the importance of donations, both financial and organ!

Start a letter-writing campaign. Use that address book like you've never used it before. Old school friends, second cousins, college roomies, send them all letters and let them know you can use their help and they can be heroes too. You can even find sample letters to get you started at www.pscpartners.org.

Last but not least, be creative. The above fundraisers are preapproved, but that's no reason you can't try for one of your own! Come up with a great idea, submit your plan and off you go!

Overachiever Effort: Are you kidding? You're going to end up on a cereal box. You're already an overachiever!

Now, for a word from our sponsor:

While you're out there saving the world, earning tons of green don't forget that it's not just funds we PSCers need to save the day. Awareness is key, so tell one and all about PSC and its devastating effects and how they can help. Don't forget organ donation awareness. Include information on how to become an organ donor since it's the ultimate heroism.

Find out more at www.pscpartners.org or at www.donatelife.net. No two ways about it. Organ Donation saves lives. So, be green. Be super. Recycle yourself.

Literally save dozens of lives all by signing up to be an organ donor and convincing those around you to be heroes too!

Save the Day: Dream a (not so little) Dream

Sandi Pearlman, The Duct, Fall 2010, pages 16-18

Do you all know the story of Rip Van Winkle, the dude who lay down to sleep and woke up some 20-100 years later (depending on the version you hear)? I've got to confess sometimes I envy old Rip. I don't want to be branded as lazy or be nagged and henpecked--and lord knows I'd hope somebody would be kind enough to put a waxer on retainer if I was going to sleep that long--but I do envy that extended blissful slumber that he got to take without a care in the world.

Then, we add to that the fact that he woke up years later to a world full of new possibilities and, wow, even the bluest of eyes might turn green. Can you imagine if that was our fate? If we could get some good quality sleep and wake up in a world where there was a cure for PSC? How amazing would that be? I mean, sure, there'd be a lot of drawbacks to missing the last 20 or so years, but we'll just suspend that reality for now, okay? :)

The thing is, unlike Rip, there's probably not some magic folklore wizard to wave his or her wand and make things happen; so it's up to us to be our own magical beings and help to shape and create the future we want to be a part of. The good news is we can most definitely do it. The better news is that now is that time!

Each October, PSC Partners sets its annual Save the Day international fundraiser into effect where we ask PSCers all over the world to step up and spread awareness and hold local fundraisers designed to let the world know we're here and that we're raising funds for a cure! The fantastic news is that we've got research grants just waiting to be funded and some of the most amazing scientific minds in the world ready and willing to delve into PSC and study the heck out of it. The even more fantastic news is that every single penny helps and FUNdraising can be done by anyone of any age. And, when we all do it together, all over the world, wow, what a difference we can make! So, whether you're in Kalamazoo, Kyoto or County Clare, now's the time to stand up and be counted. And if your energy doesn't permit you to hold your own fundraiser, garage sale, bake sale, etc. and your medical bills make donating even a few dollars impossible this year, know that we've got your back and that we know when you're once again at full speed, you'll have ours. The important thing is that together, we can accomplish anything!

Wondering what fundraisers are/have been up and running this year? Here's a quick look at some of the fun and fabulous ways PSCers are spreading the word and raising funds for a cure:

Bake Sales: Because cupcakes and cookies are popular all over the world and I'm thoroughly convinced if you present somebody with delicious baked goods they'll be on your side forever.

Garage Sales: Ever look around your home and realize that there's just too much...well, everything? A garage or yard sale lets you do yourself a favor while meeting lots of neighbors and potential new allies. Put up a sign that all money goes to charity or print out our fundraising flyer from PSC Partners (www.pscpartners.org/brochures) and spread awareness like it's going out of style. Many of our garage sale holding members have told us that they set out a donation jar as well and even when people don't purchase anything, they often donate to the cause!

Change Jar Donations: Wonder what to do with that change accumulating, well, everywhere? Leave the gumball machines to the kiddos and put your spare change to use saving lives. Collect it in a jar or get the whole family/office, etc. to drop theirs in, too and watch those pennies, quarters and dimes add up to better treatments and a cure.

Dress Down Days: It's very rare I meet anyone who doesn't love a good dress down day. I'm on disability and I still remember the reverence and awe I felt when I knew one was coming up. Dress down days are easy to set up and you'll make your coworkers eternally grateful. Like me and unable to work? Did you know that many HR departments are only too happy to help raise funds and awareness for a good cause? Ask your local companies and you may find that quite a few are willing to "jeans it up" in the name of awareness and education and to help a local community member.

Silent Auctions: Big or small in scale and with any combination of items under the sun, silent auctions are a fun way to shop for a cause. So, ask everyone to bring a white elephant item to your next dinner party and then bid on all your pals' great stuff while they bid on yours. It really is true what they say about one man's trash being another man's treasure. The last small scale silent auction I attended had only 30 people and we raised over $1,000 for PSC Partners! Want to go grander? Get your religious organizations involved, hit up your neighbors, community hangouts, local artists and friends. Let everyone know 100 percent of profits go to PSC Partners and get ready to score some great new finds.

Benefit Concerts: Have a talent that you'd like to share with the world? Whether you're a talented operatic singer like this year's concert holder or an actor who's always looking for a role or you can play a mean guitar, you can use your abilities to rock out and raise awareness and funds. Gather talented friends and colleagues and put on a performance that'll not only raise the roof but also let everyone know that PSC exists and that they can help us to find a cure all while enjoying a bit of culture!

Wine Tastings: Yes, you'd think that wine tastings and liver disease wouldn't go together; but let me tell you, they're a match made in spades, like champagne and caviar. Whether you want to go low key and host an at-home version or pair up with a local winery, wine tastings are popular ways to reach a broad audience and have mega appeal! (Caveat: I'm not advocating that wine consumption is okay for PSCers, that's between you and your docs, or at the very least you and your liver!)

Marathon Runs: Do you know how many people attend a marathon? Ask friends and family to sponsor you for miles, put SuperLiver right on your jersey—do marathoners wear jerseys? In any case, while doing your thing, you can advertise to runners, bystanders and, maybe if you're lucky, local TV and/or radio. No matter where you place, you'll definitely be the winner in our eyes!

Firstgiving Pages: Firstgiving makes it incredibly easy to raise funds for whatever cause you choose. You can use it for birthday donations, walk/run events, in lieu of wedding gifts; the sky's the limit. Another great thing about Firstgiving fundraising, not only can you e-mail it and share it with your entire address book, your friends and family can pass on your fundraising info to all their friends and family and it only takes moments to set up. For me and for many of the other Firstgiving fundraisers I know, the last thing we needed was another coffee mug, tie, pair of fuzzy socks. Through Firstgiving pages, we felt all the love and the funds donated do so much more good than even the best box of chocolates or the most gorgeous blooms!

Advertisements/Publicity: Talk to your local papers, newsletters, community events coordinators, you name it. You never know who would be willing to run a story on you and PSC or PSC Partners. Tell them the truth about what life is like living with a too little known chronic, incurable illness and give every reader the information they need to be a part of PSC Partners' grant funding from the comfort of their own homes. Wouldn't it be amazing to inform and empower all those people in your own neighborhoods while they're browsing their morning papers or checking out their favorite news site online? Just one or two clicks and they can "Donate Now" right on our homepage at: www.pscpartners.org.

These are just a few of this year's fundraisers. There are so many more and the best part is it's not only easy and fun, it makes a real difference. So many of us feel at a loss with our diagnosis, we feel we're living a nightmare and that the power has been taken from us, our lives and our loved ones. It's time to take that power back. We can't let the days pass us like they did old Rip Van Winkle, as much as we might crave a nap that would make cats around the world jealous. Finding and funding a cure doesn't have to be just a dream! Can you imagine if we all just took one weekend, one week or one month to work together to broadcast our plight and raise funds? It's not just a dream, it's happening and it's never too late to join in.

Save the Day runs through the end of November, so check back next issue to learn how this year's fundraisers went and some of the lowdown on what we loved doing, what we think everyone should do and what we now realize we were just plain old crazy to attempt. All that and early returns that'll give us an idea of just how many research grants we can fund! Sounds pretty dreamy, right?

Don't forget to check out Shop PSC Partners Seeking a Cure to purchase great gifts, mementos and more! Shopping while helping to fund a cure for PSC, how can you possibly beat that? :)

To all of this year's fundraisers, thank you for making 2010's PSC Partners Save the Day absolutely rock. We're inspired by your creativity and determination and awed by your dedication. In fact, we just couldn't dream up better folks to be in the trenches with. Thank you for reminding us we're not all alone out there and for making sure that researchers the world over find discoveries that keep them up at night pondering the fantastic possibilities. . . .

NEW THIS YEAR---JUST FOR CONFERENCE FIRST-TIMERS!!!
The Duct, Winter 2011, page 17

We've set up a Friday afternoon 30-Minute Newcomer Orientation exclusively for those attending our conference for the first time.

Get the scoop on who's who, an overview of the medical presentations you'll hear, learn about our dot ID system, what to wear, and ask the questions you might be reluctant to ask in front of the larger group.

The whirlwind session will give you a chance to meet other first-timers and get a head start on a positive conference experience.

Attention all 20 and 30-Something PSCers (or those nearly in that range!) and Facebook Fans:
The Duct, Fall 2008, page 9

If you haven't already, now is a great time to join the PSC Partners Facebook page! Get in touch with other PSC-ers your age to share concerns, ask questions and discuss what life is like when you're young and diagnosed with PSC. If you've ever needed a place to complain about the fact that you need to nap when all your friends want to do is go out and party, share how you deal with drinking, ask others about issues dealing with starting a family, etc., here's the place for you! To join, simply log onto www.Facebook.com and follow the prompts to set up a free account. It's simple to do and just takes minutes. Once you have your account, just type in PSC Partners in the search box under Groups and you'll be taken to the page. It's just that easy! Hope to see and hear from you soon!

Sandi Pearlman's Tribute to Philip Burke
Facebook, September 24, 2013 and The Duct, December 2013, pages 4-5

There is a Philip Burke-shaped hole in the Universe. And I confess, I don't quite know how to get through the days and hours without him. Right now, I can't even seem to get through a two-hour stretch without dissolving into tears. He was my friend, my confidant, my protector, my brother, my co-moderator, my fellow PSCer and so much more. We talked or texted multiple times a day on most days and knew many of the intricacies of each other's lives, schedules and activities; and we always had each other's backs. I was incredibly lucky to have him as one of my closest friends and to be able to tell him how much he meant to me on a regular basis. Wherever he may be, I know he knows how much I love him and that he's left his handprint on my heart as permanent as India ink and will always be with me. I am a better me because of my friendship with him.

I know many of you feel much the same way, that the world just isn't the same without Philip Burke in it. You're right. The world isn't ever going to be the same. But let's make it different in a way that would matter to Philip. Let's honor him by doing what we do best here, talking about PSC and all of its attending necessities and supporting each other throughout this journey. Let's raise our voices and talk about the need for organ donation. Let's raise research funds to help those scientists unlock every single piece of this puzzle. Let's band together and honor Philip and all those others we've lost, some far too recently and some far too long ago. Let's make a difference and let's be there for each other, because sometimes the best medicine in the world is having somebody who really, truly understands what we're going through by our sides.

I'll miss Philip every single day for as long as I draw breath. It's not often one finds a friend like him. Having him in my life was a gift and I know that if there's a choir in Heaven, and that's where he is, that they're celebrating Philip and his voice and spirit. I truly believe the stars are shining brighter knowing he's up there amongst them. I know you'll miss Philip, too, and please know that with each posting about your day or your health, whether posting up a picture of yourself living life to the fullest or asking a PSC question, you're not only making a difference for other PSCers, you're honoring him. So thank you for being part of PSC Partners Facebook and thank you for the outpouring of support and sorrow you've shared, because it takes strength to say we're scared and feeling a bit less sure of the Universe. I've never quite seen anything like the outpouring of love for Philip on these boards and in the private messages you've sent me. I know it means the world to me and to Philip's family as well. And we'll know that with each posting, the subtext between the lines is love and respect for Philip and a desire to bring about an end to PSC.

PSC Partners Facebook Support Group Page
Accessed October 9, 2014

This site is for all PSCers & their caregivers. Please respect everyone on the site. We may be different, but we're all in this together! As a reminder, this Facebook group is an open group. This means that the information you choose to share on this group may be publicly available to non-members of the group including friends, family, employers, prospective employers, insurance companies, and anyone else you would imagine that would be interested in your personal health care information. Please do not post anything that you would not be comfortable sharing publicly.

We're thrilled you chose to join us here and to be a part of our group. It's our privilege to help provide information & education resources for PSCers & their caregivers worldwide. For those who'd like to belong to more than one support group, here are some options:

PSCP Closed Group - http://tinyurl.com/PSCPClosedGroup

. . . . - ***below is the reasoning for the open group, as stated in the words of Sandi, who created both FB support groups***

Every time I post here, I raise awareness of PSC not only by sharing my story here with those who have PSC, but also those who can read about it on my newsfeed, etc (which I've allowed via my privacy settings). I'm also making a statement saying that this is me and I will not let my illness control what I say and where, etc. I won't hide it no matter what or from whom. My choice isn't for everyone, but for me, that makes a difference, knowing I'm doing my part to get the word out there and to say I have this; it doesn't make me less; and to be very up front about PSC and what it has brought/taken, etc. There's absolutely no judgment for anyone who doesn't want to share that way because certainly many people might not, but for me, that's part of it.

Another part is that more than a few PSC doctors and researchers have mentioned to me how much they learn from this group about what's going on with the PSC population, things they may not have realized were "bigger" than one or two PSCers, etc. So, it's about that, too, letting the PSC researchers and doctors have access to what really concerns us.

Another very large piece for me is that I feel strongly (again, my opinion) that there shouldn't be a barrier to getting information, particularly with something as rare and still largely unheard of as PSC. Sometimes PSCers and caregivers need to lurk for a bit in order to feel comfortable enough to post or to jump in and feel comfortable sharing their stories, etc. And with this Open group, a PSCer or caregiver can find us, read what's going on with our community, access our Files tab with tons of great information, etc. and then join only when and if they're ready to post or when they're ready. Whether that takes them 3 hours, 3 days, 3 months or 3 years, it doesn't matter. The information is there for them when and how they need it. For the closed group, they'd first have to ask to join before they can see anything and sometimes getting and dealing with a diagnosis of PSC is all somebody can take and, even though it may sound silly, asking to join a group sight unseen, may just be too much to take on at any given moment.

And, last but not least, closed groups are still online groups, so I guess I don't figure one is "safer" than another in any way. Truthfully, no matter where we post, if somebody really wants our information they can get to it. For those who want to keep things out of their newsfeeds or have stricter privacy settings, etc., though, the closed group may be a really good option for at least some of their questions and posts.

Open or Closed group, both are run by PSC Partners Seeking a Cure and Philip and myself. We encourage everyone to participate in either or both PSC Partners groups and to post wherever and however often they choose. There really is no right or wrong. It's just all about preferences. And, as always, Philip and I are also always more than happy to post questions up for members who want to send us private messages and would like to ask a question that they don't want linked back to them for any reason whatsoever (we won't even ask why). It's never a problem for us to do that and we absolutely keep confidentiality (we've even signed documents to that effect, so there's no worries!)

Hope this makes sense! Whichever group feels or fits best, whether that's one or the other or both, we're just happy everyone is here and sharing and making each other's lives that much better by reminding us we're all in this together, no matter what. Knowing you all are out there has been amazing for both Philip and myself and, we hope, for everyone here as well!

Hope this helps explain things a bit, at least from my point of view. Sandi Pearlman

The Happiness Plan
Sandi Pearlman, The Duct, Fall 2009, pages 8-11

By now, even the man in the moon knows my mantra of "If it's got to be laugh or cry, pick laugh," and he's even getting ready to tell me to shut the, ahem, heck up as I repeat it to myself maniacally in doctor's offices, waiting rooms, at the supermarket, basically whenever life hands me a problem that I just don't feel equipped to handle, you know, like waking up.

Sure, some might consider it a personality disorder at this point, but I prefer to think of it much more like Ally McBeal's dancing baby or internal theme song, a reminder of something that I want that's eventually going to be within my reach. (And, yes, I'm fully aware that many of you are too young to remember Ally. Go rent the DVDs, trust me on this, you'll enjoy it.) But I think internal theme songs and stupid sitcoms and rocking out with your hairbrush in bed (or the hallway a la Tom Cruise--yeah, I'm old, check out *Risky Business*) are the things that make life more livable. PSC has taken so much control of so many of our lives. I think it's time we take some power back. I think we should make a group pledge.

Place your hand(s) over your hearts. I'll wait. I see you there in the papasan: hands up! This is important. Repeat after me, "I vow to do one thing every single day to make myself ridiculously happy." There was that so hard? And for those of you with roommates, spouses, children or animals who are now looking at you like you're a nutter, admit it, looking at their confused faces is sort of enjoyable, right?

So, how do we get to this great beacon of happiness on the days where PSC has positively screwed cheer? It's not that hard or complicated. Think about it, what makes you giggle? Feel beautiful or handsome or hot? What makes you forget, even for a second, about your PSC and upcoming colonoscopies and itching and RUQ pain?

Well, for me, that's largely anesthesia (which I am completely in love with. You know how some women fantasize about marrying doctors or lawyers or cowboys? I think my fantasy involves an anesthesiologist who quite literally can take me away from all of this madness. But I guess that's between me and my therapist, right?) Anyhow, here are some tried and true happiness guaranteed suggestions. Find one you like. Steal it. Wanna try one on? Borrow it. Have one of your own. Go for it!

Guaranteed Happiness Plan # 1:

On days when fatigue won't let you get out of bed, give in. Make a day of it. Every once in a bit, let the fatigue monster win, but on your terms. Cuddle up under a generous comforter (there's a reason they're called that) and watch some bad TV or pop your favorite DVD into the laptop or player. Wanna wallow? *Terms of Endearment, Hancock and An Affair to Remember* work for me.

I have a guy friend who denies it but ALWAYS cries at the ends of *Rent* and *Titanic*. *Marley and Me* and *Steel Magnolias* are good choices too. Want to laugh? Try *Some Like it Hot* or *Bringing Up Baby* or *Elf.* Fill in the blanks. You know you have a movie that makes you smile from ear to ear and, if you don't, might I suggest just about anything with Haley Mills?

In any case, commit yourself to the plan. It's not fatigue's or your body's choice to lie in bed all day. It's yours. You're in control and if you want to sneak a bit of ice cream or popcorn in there with you, who's going to know? And for those of you with kids or a hubby, make it an event. Bring them on in and introduce the kiddos to Mary Poppins or *The Wizard of Oz* or watch old family movies. I have no idea why, but children will sit still for HOURS just to watch themselves on TV!

Guaranteed Happiness Plan # 2:

Next time you're out and about, buy yourself a coloring book of your choice and the good pack of crayons. You know which ones I'm talking about, the yellow and green box that has the sharpener built into the back. Now, before you stop reading and decide that lack of sleep and medication have made me a loon, think about it. There's a reason why therapists use coloring as a tool to help kids work through issues.

First, it's hard to be angry or stressed or overwhelmed while you're coloring. Second, if you are any of those things, chances are that focusing on your coloring will help you sort out the issues that are bugging you or give you a safe place to vent rage: coloring Mickey Mouse a moldy green color or making Prince Charming have buck teeth can be strangely soothing.

Guaranteed Happiness Plan # 3:

Okay. I stole this one from Oprah who, I'm sure, stole it from somebody else, but, hey, she's Oprah and we all know she can get away with stuff like that. Start a happiness journal. Write down three things every single day that made you happy. I don't care if it's making a traffic light on your way to work that you usually miss, a really good Bacon, Egg and Cheese Biscuit at the local fast food place, or that your dishwasher magically unloaded itself. Whatever the reason, write it down.

I've had days where I've written down this list: (1) Didn't throw up for three hours. (2) Cat purred and gave me a kiss. (3) New episode of *The Biggest Loser* was on tonight. As you can see, it doesn't have to be earth-shattering stuff. But here's the kicker. One, I love my little happiness journal. It's brown and has a fabric fastener and looks like something Hemmingway would've had. Two, just making myself sit down at the end of the day (or continue laying down but with a pen in my hand this time) and thinking of and writing down three things that made me happy that day makes me feel like a nerd, but a happy one. And three, remember how we talked about the days when you need a good laugh, try rereading your journal. I guarantee it'll make you smile. Oh, and remember it's one of the Big O's (not that one) favorite things to do. You don't want to defy her now, do you?

Guaranteed Happiness Plan # 4:

Be honest with yourself and others. So many young PSCers I talk to want to hide their PSC away like it's a secret shame. I get that. I really do. It's such a hard thing to tell somebody or to make them understand. We want to protect those around us. We don't want to be a burden. Plus, to tell our truth, we have to think of timing and be ready for the risk of rejection and be willing to open ourselves up for judgement on something that is so much bigger than a secret stash of girlie magazines or bridal porn (which is what those of us in the industry call all of those bridal mags).

The only problem is that by hiding what is and what will always be such a large part of ourselves, we're perpetuating a myth that we're flawed and unlovable. We're telling others by our very evasiveness that we expect them to judge us and find us lacking. It's hard to bite the bullet. You might lose people who you thought were your friends. But in the end, instead of carrying around a bucket of evasions and creating a circle for yourself where there's no real support, you'll have ties that won't break.

You'll have truth instead of lies. You'll have compassion and understanding when you need it. There will be hands to hold in waiting rooms and people to celebrate real triumphs like improving LFTs and no longer looking like a banana after a fit of cholangitis and jaundice. In addition, what better way to advocate towards research and a cure than to be a walking billboard? If you don't advocate for yourself and make it known how important organ donation and funding are, who will? And how happy and fab will you feel when PSC stands for problem so cured.

Guaranteed Happiness Plan # 5:

Spoil yourself. I know belts are tightening all around these days and not just from PSC weight loss. But I urge you to make the investment in yourself.

You can treat yourself to weekly or monthly pedicures (guys, trust me, if you're thinking this suggestion is too girly, you haven't experienced the loveliness of a pedicure for badly itching feet) or buy yourself a bottle of your favorite polish and do an at-home version.

Love to read? When you have the energy, hit your local library. I'm a former librarian and to me books are the be-all/end-all. But frequent hospitalizations and travel make lugging books back and forth a trial, so I'm thinking about succumbing to one of those e-readers and thinking of the expense as one for my emotional and physical sanity.

Grab a blanket and go for a picnic in the park with the kids and count stars or cloud-spot. Run through the sprinkler in the backyard. Stop by an animal shelter and take a lonely dog for a walk. Host a potluck if you're too tired to go out to dinner. Log on to Bluefly.com or QVC or UncommonGoods.com and shop till you drop without moving much more than a finger muscle (and best of all, you don't even have to purchase anything!). Get a massage. Color your hair.

Whisk (or have your significant other whisk you) away on a romantic weekend in your own town. See a movie you've been dying to see. Designate a game night (can't go wrong with Clue, Monopoly or Scrabble in my book). Subscribe to your favorite magazine. Spend an entire day in bed watching Food TV. In short, it doesn't matter what you do, just make sure you do it and enjoy every second of it.

Guaranteed Happiness Plan # 6:

You tell me. Log on to PSC Partners Facebook (. . . then search PSC Partners to find the group) and add what makes you deliriously, wickedly, convulsively happy. Then sit back, smile and know you've done a good deed for the day, you've made someone else smile.

Spirituality
Sandi Pearlman, June 2009

We've all had them, days where we're sure we'd rather wake up dead or where even the tiniest inconvenience leads to a big explosion, maybe it's that you're too tired to finish that load of laundry, that you're itching so much that a severe case of poison oak sounds like a vacation or you're just plain old ticked waiting for biopsy results to come back. Whatever the trigger, PSC and stress go hand in hand like peanut butter and jelly on a third date. So, what are your options other than pulling out your hair, yelling at your loved ones or crying buckets? Well, there's medication, there's violence (which I don't recommend) and then there's spirituality. Now for some of you, spirituality is a hot button word. You don't want talk about religion or sitting around in heated caves in the middle of the woods while you expose your "information" to the bunnies and the bats. Not to worry, spirituality is something different for every person I've ever met and that's the good news. The better news is that it offers HUGE relief in busting stress..and that should have you unclenching those jaws and headed towards easy breathing.

So, what is spirituality then? Well, it's anything and everything that makes you feel connected and a bit freer from the everyday stressors of your world. Dictionary.com defines spirituality as: "1. The quality or state of being spiritual; incorporeality; heavenly-mindedness. A pleasure made for the soul, suitable to its spirituality. --South." What this means to us is that to achieve stress-busting spirituality it isn't necessary to set foot in a church or synagogue (although there's certainly nothing wrong with that if that's your choice), but there are a myriad of things you can do to become a bit more spiritual, whatever the term means to you. Remember, it's a "pleasure made for the soul" so whatever pleases your soul is, therefore, by definition spiritual. So, if it's sitting by a stream, dunking your toes in a pool, practicing yoga, petting your cat or a good long hug that lowers your blood pressure and takes your mind or your body to a serene place, go for it. Don't be ashamed of a good long cry (spirituality sometimes requires tears), feel free to ask for a hug. Define spirituality your way. Read a book. Take a bubble bath. Write down three things every single day that made your world a better place even if it's something as simple as "the sink is free of dirty dishes." Revel in what brings you joy and don't feel ashamed or judged. Spirituality is about pleasure and pleasure is a stress-free zone and which one of us doesn't deserve that at least once in while? So, start today. Turn off your phones, yes, all of them. Grab your hubby or your bubble bath or your dog and give spirituality a try. It's not just for organized religion or those who can bend their bodies in ways that would make a pretzel jealous. It's for you. It's for me. With PSC pleasure doesn't often figure in, so why not create some where you can? Make PSC stand for Pressure-free, Spirituality, Contentment at least for a few hours a week. After all, what do you have to lose?

National Center for Advancing Translational Sciences

The NIH/NCATS GRDR℠ Program
Global Rare Diseases Patient Registry
Data Repository

Who are you? A Primary Sclerosing Cholangitis (PSC) Story- GRDR participant

Who are you? Really, think about it before you answer. Who are you? Did you answer with what you do? Librarian, teacher, dentist, you name it? The specifics don't matter, just the identity exercise. Who are you? So often that's answered as if the question was asked, "What do you do?" For those of us with chronic illness, invisible and visible, who are we? What do we do? What are we in a world that defines itself by what our bodies are able to do or not able to do every single day?

I'm a million different things. I bet you are, too. But I have an illness, one that most people have never heard about; one that most doctors have never heard about. It's incurable, has no viable treatments, can strike anyone at any time; and, often, it's one that is invisible to the naked eye. I have Primary Sclerosing Cholangitis, PSC. It's a rare, incurable disease of the liver and bile ducts that changes the way I have to live my life every single day. I itch as though somebody poured itching powder in my bloodstream and then shoved me into an endless pile of fire ants. I'm nauseous. I have pain every single day and my brain and body can no longer function the way they used to. My exhaustion is so pervasive that it's mental, physical and emotional. Even my skin color is different. I live inside a body that I can't even recognize most days and, yet, to the casual observer, I may look healthy. I get dirty looks when I use my handicapped pass in parking lots even though often by the time I've gotten from the car to the front of the store I'm too tired to accomplish my task.

I'm no longer who I used to be. I'm no longer a librarian or a driver or somebody who can run a mile. But I'm a warrior. I'm a fighter and an educator. I'm unafraid to say I have PSC or to take the time to explain to a physician or a bystander what it is. I shout my differences in the name of education and awareness. I teach others not to judge by sight alone. I teach them to listen and help them to find compassion and to want to cure me, to cure those like me. I show those with my disease that they are not alone and that we're in this together. I'm not a victim. I'm a survivor. And if my disease takes me tomorrow, it will be on my terms and because I've taught what I've needed to teach and I've said what needed to be said. It will be because my body can no longer take being "other," finding itself inflicted with a disease that very few know and that its resources cannot fight off. It will be because my soul has more work to do than my tired physique can support. And yet, should that happen, I won't cease to exist. Who I was, what I did, those questions may still be asked. The answers? My answers? More researchers and doctors and civilians will know the name PSC and will realize there is a war to win than before I came. Who am I? I'm me of course, bum liver, devastating disease and all. Who are you?

Sandi Pearlman is the Community Relations Chair for PSC Partners Seeking a Cure, a 501(c)3 dedicated to raising education, and awareness of PSC while raising research funds to find better treatments and a cure. She started a mentor program to help PSCers all over the world connect and created an international support group for the organization . . . To find out more about PSC, go to: www.pscpartners.org.